Major League Soccer 2019

Shane Stay

MAJOR LEAGUE
SOCCER
2019

Fountaindale Public Library
Bolingbrook, IL
(630) 759-2102

Everything You Need to
Know About the Teams

Meyer & Meyer Sport

British Library Cataloguing in Publication Data
A catalogue record for this book is available from the British Library

Major League Soccer 2019
Maidenhead: Meyer & Meyer Sport (UK) Ltd., 2019
ISBN: 978-1-78255-159-1

© 2019 by Meyer & Meyer Sport (UK) Ltd.
Aachen, Auckland, Beirut, Cairo, Cape Town, Dubai, Hägendorf, Hong Kong, Indianapolis,
Manila, New Delhi, Singapore, Sydney, Tehran, Vienna

Member of the World Sports Publishers' Association (WSPA), www.w-s-p-a.org
Printed by CM Books, Ann Arbor, MI, USA
ISBN: 978-1-78255-159-1
Email: info@m-m-sports.com
www.thesportspublisher.com

CONTENTS

INTRODUCTION

MLS: The world's next super league. It's as simple as that. There are already established leagues that seem irreplaceable: English Premier League, Bundesliga, Serie A, La Liga. Can MLS do it? Can MLS reach the mountaintop, and become as powerful as these leagues? Many people say yes.

Essentially, an elite league is defined by quality of play and profitability.

As the leader in world athletics, the United States is simply the place to be for other leagues, including the NBA, NHL, and MLB.* Players from all around the world want to play in these leagues; it's their ultimate destination. In part, this is what MLS is striving for, to be an ultimate destination for any soccer player.

---

*   The NFL, one of America's top leagues, cannot be considered in this respect because American football is essentially a niche sport; very few countries around the world partake in the game. Although many Americans view it as the sport of all sports—and it very well might be—it's still a niche sport, almost exclusively restricted to America's borders. (The Canadian Football League mainly uses American players, and the now-defunct NFL Europe mainly used American players.) With that said, the NFL does draw athletes from other countries from time to time.

MLS wants to be one of the world's top soccer leagues, and one of America's top athletic leagues, both in terms of quality of play and profitability. It wants to be on par with the EPL, Bundesliga, Serie A, La Liga, and the elite leagues of Europe, along with the NBA, NFL, NHL, and MLB, the powerhouse leagues within the American sports landscape. In some respects, this is occurring as we speak; MLS is pulling in higher attendance for live games than some NBA and NHL franchises, though TV ratings for MLS games are not quite as high as its American counterparts.

And this is the tricky thing about MLS. It's not just competing with soccer leagues around the world, it's also competing with sports in America. The other international soccer leagues have a few distinct advantages over MLS. For starters, most, if not all, soccer leagues have been around a lot longer than MLS. Also, soccer is the favorite sport of many countries. Soccer is on the rise in America—some think it's soon to replace baseball in popularity—but it's not the most popular sport. Therefore, MLS is competing with other established sports in America, such as the Big 3 (i.e., baseball, basketball, and football). Of course, European nations have other competing sports, but soccer is far and away their favorite pastime. Essentially, MLS is pleading with Americans to choose soccer over other established sports in a way that's different from European nations and, for that matter, pretty much every other nation on earth.

Organizers of American soccer (including but not limited to US Soccer, along with the leaders of MLS) see this quest of getting MLS to be an elite world-class league as something within the realm of possibility. With a late start, the US is on its way to dominating the world's game, soccer.† (To people that might laugh at this idea, proceed with caution; the US has dominated the Olympics for years, and soccer is quite literally America's last athletic frontier. The US will dominate soccer as well, someday. *When* is the question.) Attaining world soccer supremacy includes winning the World Cup (a process patriotically occurring by continental drift) and making MLS an elite league. Both these quests are very attainable, and the latter is currently underway. Without a doubt, it's a top-shelf priority, and, if MLS organizers have anything to say about it, it will happen. Currently, they're in a good place; Major League Soccer has turned into a great success.

In 2017, Ken Belson wrote a story for *The New York Times* that described some of the process for choosing expansion franchises for MLS (this was prior to Nashville, Tennessee being accepted into the league). Don Garber—the Commissioner of Major League Soccer—was touring Nashville, weighing his options, meeting with officials, and receiving first-class hospitality. (At this point, there were other cities eager to join MLS, including Detroit, Indianapolis, and St. Louis.) Ken Belson wrote, "So for Garber, who stood at the lectern in Nashville, the latest warm reception seemed as much a validation as an opportunity. He had taken over a struggling 12-team league in 1999 and contracted

---

†   At times, American soccer almost seems complacent with its place among the world's soccer giants. Yet, there is an American drive to seek the mountaintop. Along the way, bad decisions have been made here and there, but the intent is to rise up and meet the challenge. This is where MLS plays a very important role as a place for players to gain vital top-level experience, which has been lacking in past years.

it to 10 clubs two years later to stave off its collapse. Now, the league is executing a plan to grow to 28 clubs by 2020, and interest in professional soccer in the United States—in M.L.S. and far beyond it—has surged."[1]

For all intents and purposes, there's no looking back. MLS is crackling with energy, leaving many to extrapolate its future rise to power, on par with the EPL and Serie A. It wasn't always that way. Originally, there were fears that MLS would not make it, that it wouldn't expand, that it would be an ephemeral soccer dream for American soccer dreamers, much like the NASL. And, guess what? MLS might not make it. There is always a chance that it might fold, though it seems highly likely that it will succeed. As of 2018, there were 23 teams in MLS. As the league transitions from 2018 to 2019, even though TV viewership of games is not as high as it could be, MLS games are filling stadiums left and right, and more teams are jumping on board, including franchises in Miami, Cincinnati, and Nashville, ready to take off.

Typically, MLS attendance per game is greater than NBA or NHL games. This is amazing considering people still don't think of soccer as being on par with the NBA or NHL. But MLS is winning American hearts with mascots like Kingston in Orlando, a man dressed up like a lion who hangs out with fans, and in Portland, a tree is literally carved up with a chainsaw every time a goal is scored by the home side.

The MLS season lasts from March to October,‡ a nice window of opportunity to avoid conflicts with the major American sports landscape, mainly the basketball and football seasons. As a result,

---

‡   The MLS season schedule can potentially change.

MLS competes more with the baseball season, giving viewers a healthy alternative to watching men stand around on a baseball diamond, who in turn watch other men throw a ball, swing a bat, and potentially run. (Who doesn't love baseball? Yet, over the years, Americans have reluctantly conceded how boring it can potentially be.)

Unlike in England and other places, there is no relegation in MLS. In this regard, MLS is like the other major American sports (i.e., baseball, basketball, football, and hockey). The teams remain in the league from season to season.

But MLS is very different from other major American sports in that it is fighting for its place in the hierarchy of world soccer leagues. For their respective sports, the NFL, NBA, NHL, and MLB are the places to be. They're the equivalent of the English Premiere League, the Bundesliga, La Liga, and Serie A. Obviously, without question, MLS wants to meet the standard of European soccer. And one day MLS should get there.

Sometimes it's easy to forget that MLS is just a baby league, with so much potential. Many club teams of Europe—such as AC Milan—have been around since the late 1800s while MLS made its first appearance in 1996! Therefore, Europe has quite a head start. But this is part of the struggle and challenge that MLS has accepted. MLS is very American in that it's up against the odds, and it needs something very spectacular to pull off a miraculous victory. Like the US hockey team of 1980 facing the USSR, it's a *league out of its league* with other leagues that have way too much experience, star power, money, and prestige. The fact that MLS has expanded into a vibrant league with fan bases like Portland and Seattle that rival any English club at their most passionate is quite a success.

HISTORY OF MAJOR LEAGUE SOCCER

There is a long path of soccer history leading up to Major League Soccer. It didn't just appear out of nowhere. There have been other leagues before it that are worth exploring.

PROFESSIONAL INDOOR SOCCER IN THE UNITED STATES: A BRIEF HISTORY

Before we get into MLS and the outdoor professional soccer leagues of the US, it's important to point out how indoor soccer has provided a strong presence for professional soccer in the country.

Since 1978, believe it or not, there has been professional indoor soccer in the United States, which has survived under different names including the Major Indoor Soccer League (MISL), the National Professional Soccer League (NPSL), the World Indoor Soccer League (WISL), the National Indoor Soccer League (NISL), the Professional Arena Soccer League (PASL), and the Major Arena Soccer League (MASL). These leagues have provided a competitive professional outlet for players from around the world, the most well-known being the MISL which had a huge following from the 70s into the mid 80s, wherein arenas were consistently sold out with passionate fans. Many of the sellouts were for regular season games, not just the playoffs. There were extravagant pre-game introductions, many of which came across like rock concerts. It was a league that appeared to be the next big thing in American sports. The games were exciting and action-packed, with plenty of goals, led by star players including but not limited to Branko Šegota, Steve Zungul, Daryl Doran, Tatu, and Preki.

Over the years, however, the indoor scene wavered in popularity. Despite this trend, it has been a regular presence for professional soccer in America, and it continues to exist.

Indoor soccer is important for a number of reasons. It increases touches on the ball, allowing players to improve their skill level in games. It is arguably more difficult to play than outdoor soccer as it demands more skill and endurance. For any individual, indoor soccer provides an important platform to become better as a player. In essence, playing indoor soccer improves an individual player's skillset for the outdoor game. However, over the years, it was very difficult for the US men's national team to improve its quality of play given that indoor soccer was the only reliable professional soccer league in the US. Indoor soccer provided a place to compete, but it's different than outdoor soccer. Just as indoor soccer is necessary to improve any player's game, having *only* indoor as a professional outlet was not good for the overall experience of national team players to translate their indoor experience to the outdoor game.

Throughout the years, and definitely prior to 1996 (when MLS was introduced), there was a conscious awareness from the American soccer community that in order for soccer to improve in America, the United States needed to establish a legitimate outdoor league, something the rest of the world already had in place.

PROFESSIONAL OUTDOOR SOCCER IN THE UNITED STATES: A BRIEF HISTORY

Prior to Major League Soccer, there have been a number of professional and semi-professional soccer leagues in the United States.

From 1967 until 1985, the NASL (North American Soccer League) was the biggest success.[2] It was a league which acquired the services of Pelé, Beckenbauer, Cruyff, Best, and others; a league which, in fact, had an interesting run, particularly in the mid to late 70s when Pelé filled stadiums around the country, energizing soccer crowds and making soccer cool. Pelé had taken world soccer to new heights, playing over a decade with Santos, the Brazilian club he was very loyal to. Then he was lured to America. Pelé, known throughout the world as the king of soccer, signed with the New York Cosmos for a three-year, $7 million contract (approximately $2 million of that amount was to pay his taxes), making him the highest-paid team athlete in the world.[3]

After Pelé left the NASL, there were some highs, the league tried to achieve greatness, but eventually it fizzled out until the 1990s. The process of taking American soccer from the passing of the NASL to the next phase in its progression was a clumsy one. From 1984 to 1996, it was finding its way; there were attempts to resuscitate the NASL or something like it, but nothing really took hold. It took a little time before MLS saved the day.

As we approach 2020, there are a few pro soccer leagues in the US. They fall under the jurisdiction of the USSF (United States Soccer Federation)—also known as US Soccer, based in Chicago, Illinois—which is the official governing body of the sport of soccer in the United States.[4]

Of course, America's top outdoor league is Major League Soccer (MLS). Below it in recent years have been the United Soccer League (USL) and the North American Soccer League (NASL). These leagues represent a historical effort by US soccer enthusiasts, which dates back many years, to make soccer a real force in America and the world.

MLS represents a long legacy of efforts to create a firm league in America. The American passion for creating a league goes all the way back to 1921 and the American Soccer League, followed by the NASL during the Pelé era, and then the indoor soccer craze; eventually, finally, MLS came into existence.

THE PATH OF MAKING SOCCER COOL IN AMERICA

You have to go all the way back to 1993, the year MLS was founded. The first games weren't played until 1996, and during that year 10 teams represented the new league.

The Original Eastern Conference (1996)

Tampa Bay Mutiny
D.C. United
New York/New Jersey MetroStars
Columbus Crew
New England Revolution

The Original Western Conference (1996)

Los Angeles Galaxy
Dallas Burn
Kansas City Wiz
San Jose Clash
Colorado Rapids

From 1996-2008, the MLS Cup championship game was televised by ABC. From 2009-2015, the championship game was televised by ESPN. In 2016, the championship game was televised by Fox before returning to ESPN in 2017. The largest attendance for an MLS Cup championship game was in 2002, with 61,316 spectators watching the match between LA Galaxy and New England Revolution at Gillette Stadium in Foxborough, Massachusetts.

Without a doubt, television coverage is important. As crazy as it sounds, prior to the 1990s, it was a difficult task to get soccer games—of practically any kind, be it domestic or from around the world—televised by ESPN or one of the major networks. So to have MLS games regularly televised is a big deal in America. It's great for the sport, and for the growth of MLS down the road.

The goal of MLS, and that of any league, is to be the best in the world. Indications show that that may be the case someday soon for Major League Soccer. Things have been very good. There's expansion. Attendance has been good. In fact, for the most part, an average game brings in more fans than an average NBA game. Soccer keeps getting more popular in the United States. Someday, very soon, it's possible MLS could be on par with the English Premiere League and Serie A.

In the beginning, however, back in the 1990s, things were very challenging for Major League Soccer. It was really about the culture of American sports and how to get soccer into that culture. That was the struggle for MLS. It was a culture that favored the Big 3 (i.e., baseball, basketball, and football). This is partially why America is so unique, and why the challenge of MLS was so great. It's important to remember that in most every other country in the world, soccer isn't just cool, it's larger than life; it's like a religion. And, for some reason, many Americans have held a certain animosity toward soccer for many years, often dismissing it as a foreign game played by foreigners. They just haven't wanted to embrace it…at all. I can recall growing up, playing youth soccer, and seeing some of the dads—men who had given their lives over to the Big 3; men who reluctantly allowed their sons to play soccer; men who watched the games, but did so with a sneer, along with much skepticism—reassuring themselves that soccer was good for one thing: to keep their boys in shape for other sports.

But then there were other men who lived by the Big 3 yet saw the potential and beauty in soccer; men like former Dallas Cowboys coach, the Texas legend, the Super Bowl champ, Tom Landry, who appreciated soccer and knew it was a legitimate sport.

The challenge of MLS was to make soccer—and the idea of a legitimate league—acceptable to mainstream America, to make soccer cool. The competition MLS faced consisted of baseball, basketball, football, NASCAR, hockey, and tennis, just to name a few.

As we approach 2020, soccer is in a battle for popularity on TV. A piece from Norman Chad in *The Washington Post* from 2018 pointed out that "taped poker—*taped poker!*—often outdraws live soccer."[5] American viewing habits can be very curious. After all, believe it or not, prior to the 80s, bowling was one of the most popular sports on TV. You know that when people prefer watching poker, NASCAR, and even bowling to watching soccer, you've got a situation on your hands. But Americans are a mysterious people, and we also allow shows like *Jersey Shore* and *Vanderpump Rules* to become sensations. This is all the more proof that if those shows can make it, there has to be a place for American soccer too.

Reality shows aside, soccer has many competitors in America, particularly with the increase in the amount of channels people have to watch (which really started to take off in the 1990s and 2000s). And most certainly, back in the late 1990s, the challenge was how to make soccer cool in order to make MLS survive.

COOL OR NOT COOL?

The first few years of MLS were a struggle. For starters, Americans were being told by advocates of MLS that soccer was cool, but the general public was unsure as to whether this was true or not. Although the United States had just hosted the 1994 World

Cup, which set records for total attendance for all World Cups, many Americans weren't sure about soccer. Cool? Not cool? Many people were not sold.

For the most part, diehard soccer fans were on board, that's for sure. But MLS needed to bring in new fans; it wanted to expand its viewership to a wider American audience.

Here's some context for what the sports world was like around the inception of MLS:

- The NBA—the hippest league in the US at the time—was witnessing a great run by the Chicago Bulls and Michael Jordan, who was riding the wave of excitement from the 80s, the decade that represented a new world of basketball which he helped create, along with the likes of Magic Johnson and Larry Bird, a rivalry that dominated the 80s and took basketball to new levels.
- The NFL was soaring as well, coming off a rush of excitement from the 1980s, with many classic teams including the San Francisco 49ers, led by Joe Montana and Jerry Rice; during this time, the NFL was becoming more of a passing league, which made the game more exciting. As the 90s progressed, the 49ers and Dallas Cowboys were front and center, primetime.
- Tennis in the 80s was spectacular with players like John McEnroe and Jimmy Connors, and then in the 90s with Andre Agassi, Pete Sampras, and Michael Chang.
- The NHL was booming from the Wayne Gretzky era in the 80s, along with the rise of Brett Hull, Jeremy Roenick, and others, and the league continued to surge into the 90s.

Then in 1996, just two years after the 1994 World Cup, MLS arrived on the scene, and right out of the gate they were offering Alexi Lalas vs. John Harkes. But it just wasn't the same. It wasn't cool enough. Make no mistake, both Lalas and Harkes were highly decorated players from college, they played in the World Cup, and they also had experience playing for European club teams, but they weren't going to bring home television ratings like Gretzky, Jordan, McEnroe, Montana, Shaq, Favre, or Deion Sanders would, and therefore MLS lacked the excitement that the NBA, NFL, and NHL brought to the table.

There were early jitters for the league. Would it last? Would it grow to the level of excitement that it has today, with outwardly passionate soccer cities, such as Portland, that embrace soccer, and have made MLS a way of life? The answers to these questions were unknown in the early days. To counter this problem, MLS promoters had a few tricks up their sleeve. They presented top-notch players like Marco Etcheverry, but the response—even from savvy American soccer fans—was, "Who?" "He's from where? Peru?" "No. *Bolivia.*" Yeah, everybody knows the powerhouse of South American soccer is none other than Bolivia! (To anyone new to soccer, that was sarcasm.) Furthermore, the traditional order of South American soccer countries, from best to last, would go something like Brazil, Argentina, Uruguay, Chile, Colombia, and then maybe Peru or Bolivia (along with Paraguay, Venezuela, and Ecuador). Nothing against Etcheverry—he was a very good player—but he just wasn't going to carry the league to new heights. Etcheverry and others were not worldwide names, and that was a problem for MLS.

During the first few years of MLS, the top players in the world were Zidane, Ronaldo, Rivaldo, Beckham, Veron, Ortega, and a young Henry, but they were spoken for. They were the Michael Jordans of their respective sport, and top teams from Europe and South America utilized their services. MLS, which became known as a retirement lot for international stars, would have to wait for Beckham and Henry, just part of the struggle Major League Soccer encountered in the early days.

So, without a doubt, in the late 90s, Major League Soccer had a challenge on its hands.

LACK OF STAR POWER

MLS is still coping with this dilemma, the issue of how to bring in more star players. In this respect, MLS is not alone. It's an issue that many leagues deal with all the time. Star players bring in other good players, more revenue, and good results. But, past and present, MLS sees itself as more than a retirement lot for international talent. By comparison with the rest of the soccer-playing world—the old guard, if you will—MLS is a new league, one with potential and on a mission to prove itself.

Especially in the early days, the lack of star power was a big hurdle for MLS to overcome. The league had good players—such as Matthaus (a big star, but not to Americans) and Donadoni (who, like Matthaus, was a star, but not a huge one in the eyes of Americans)—but it was missing a true worldwide star that would put the league over the top. Though, even with Pelé on the New York Cosmos, the NASL didn't last, which many people remembered, and this was reason for concern in regard to MLS. On top of that, the stars MLS did acquire were toward the end of their careers.

One way to counter this was to create star players from within the United States, an idea which falls in line with the Homegrown Player Rule, established in 2008, which allows teams to sign players that have been brought up within the ranks of a particular club. Often referred to as development academies, teams have a hand in training local youth players; the process of training players from within a club's system and then signing them can help propagate more local talent which is good for each club, because their youth players will be accustomed to the style of play that is expected of them once they get signed and play with the first team.

STADIUMS

Another reason MLS struggled early on was simple: stadiums. The original 10 MLS stadiums were very large for a new soccer league, in a country hesitant to embrace the sport. For the most part, MLS teams were playing in huge NFL stadiums, or something very similar. (The San Jose Clash provided the smallest venue, Spartan Stadium.)

The following are the original stadiums that were used and their seating capacities.

Original MLS Stadiums

Colorado Rapids
Mile High Stadium
76,273

Columbus Crew
Ohio Stadium
102,329

D.C. United
RFK Memorial Stadium
46,000

Dallas Burn
Cotton Bowl
92,100

Kansas City Wiz
Arrowhead Stadium
81,425

LA Galaxy
Rose Bowl
92,542

New England Revolution
Foxboro Stadium
60,292

New York/New Jersey MetroStars
Giants Stadium
80,200

San Jose Clash
Spartan Stadium
30,456

Tampa Bay Mutiny
Houlihan's Stadium
74,301

The problem was that not enough people were showing up for games which made embarrassing optics on TV. In Kansas City, for example, it's just really hard to get over 80,000 people in seats for a regular season game. The same went for other teams around the league.

For a fledgling league trying to exist, 15,000-30,000 people at a game is a huge success, but in a stadium that holds approximately 80,000 people, it looks pathetic. Soccer was being pitched to the American public as a big deal, yet when people would flip past a game on TV they'd see empty stadiums. With few exceptions, the stadiums just couldn't fill capacity. It was a lot to ask for regular season games. Also, for the most part, the lines from the football fields were shared on the soccer field, creating the headache-causing visual of two fields overlapping onto one as a soccer game was being played. Manchester United, Real Madrid, and Bayern Munich were not sharing fields with a football or rugby team; ostensibly, MLS was the only major league in the world doing such a thing. It became apparent that soccer-specific stadiums needed to be constructed, and quickly. For all teams, such a venture would have been exceedingly risky from the start. Financially, building stadiums is a big undertaking. The original MLS banked on using NFL stadiums and hoping for the best, but this was unrealistic. Eventually, MLS would succeed and expand, and soccer specific stadiums would come about (which was a big relief), but in the early days, this was definitely a drawback.

REGULAR PRESENCE ON TV

A regular presence on TV was tough. During the early years of MLS, games on TV were not as readily available as they are today. This had been a problem for the NASL, and it was still an issue. ESPN was slow to embrace soccer as a viable option. Commentators would openly mock it during highlights, or they'd reluctantly relay a news report, heavy with skepticism or sarcasm. There was always a strange hatred toward soccer. Many Americans wouldn't accept it. They wanted it to go away, or to eradicate it completely. (See "Americans Against Soccer" in the appendix for more information.)

QUALITY OF PLAY

MLS and American teams have been attacked by the rest of the world for not playing a good style. This is partly true, and it also has something to do with the rest of the world trying to hold on to the last sport they have against the United States. After all, the US has dominated the Olympics and every other sport on earth; the last athletic frontier for America is men's soccer. Therefore, many people from around the world are fearful that the US will conquer that arena too, which is why they're quick to try and keep it from succeeding. So, the easy out is to criticize the style of play.

With that said, regarding the early days of MLS (the first 10 years or so), they had a point. For a new league, the quality of play in Major League Soccer was not as good as the rest of the world. This affected attendance because fans just weren't swept off their feet by good play on the field. However, many American fans weren't equipped with good soccer radar for what was good play or not; they simply had a passion for the game. Essentially, they wanted to see the ball in the back of the net. As it turns out, this was good for MLS. The fans liked soccer regardless of style, and they began to associate with their team and felt a sense of local pride. Rivalries were formed, and things would eventually improve for MLS's success.

The American players were no less athletic than players from Europe, but there was a big drawback. Players from Europe were raised in youth farm systems. Typically, each of their professional teams had an extensive youth farm system in place, and the young players were trained so that when they got old enough and joined the first team they were ready to go. Having such a system in place creates a certain fluidity in the flow of play, which American teams are striving to reach.

The United States is the all-time leader in Olympic gold medals, which makes it the most athletic nation in the world. Whether it's the summer or winter Olympics, the US is the leader, yet there's one sport that America has yet to conquer: men's soccer. It can't be said enough: within the realm of American athletic success, it's a total enigma. Soccer has proven to be America's last athletic frontier. Based on America's overall athletic record, the men should, could, and probably will take over international soccer by winning the World Cup someday soon.* Over the years, on the international scene, soccer has been a formidable foe, especially with the lack of a viable professional outdoor league, a league

---

*   Possibly. Don't count on it, though. In fact, *soon* is the key word here. Maybe delete *soon* and just say *someday*. Yeah, that's better.

which is necessary for a national team to gain valuable experience and confidence on its quest to winning the FIFA World Cup. MLS provides a sanctuary for American players, a steady outdoor league, which results in a positive spillover effect to the national team, to reach the goal of someday winning the FIFA World Cup. Therefore, MLS plays a crucial role in the success of American soccer at the national team level.

MLS is also vital for the popularity of youth soccer in America. It gives kids a reason to play, something to strive for. Youth soccer will continue to grow in a positive direction with MLS in place.

Furthermore, the morale boost MLS brings to cities, along with financial growth in terms of jobs and the positive financial spillover effect, is great.

A LOOK BACK AT THE 2018 MLS SEASON

SOCCER RULE BOOK

The Homegrown Player Rule, established in 2008, provides a way for local players to be brought up through a team's system and signed to a contract.

The Designated Player Rule holds an interesting place in MLS. Wikipedia, the online Encyclopedia, has summed up this rule succinctly:

"The Designated Player Rule, nicknamed the Beckham Rule, was adopted as part of the salary cap regulations of Major League Soccer for the 2007 season. The rule allows each MLS franchise to sign up to three players that would be considered outside the team's salary cap (either by offering the player higher wages or by paying a transfer fee for the player), allowing MLS teams to compete for star players in the international soccer market."[6]

The offside rule continues to be "even with the last defender," though, as it has been seen from time to time, this is left to interpretation by the referees. Is it a part of the attacker's body (e.g., an arm) that is even with a part of the last defender's body?

Can this be onside? Or does it have to be a player's full body? It's up to interpretation.

Unlike American football, which seems to alter its rules from season to season, there aren't too many rule changes in soccer which is a good thing!

THE 2018 MLS ALL-STAR GAME

MLS All-Stars vs. Juventus
August 1, 2018
1-1 in regulation
3-5 in penalty kicks (winner: Juventus)
Atlanta, Georgia
Mercedes-Benz Stadium

The house was rocking but the MLS All-Stars took a close defeat to Juventus. Regulation ended in a 1-1 draw, with a goal from Josef Martinez; however, Juventus eventually won in penalty kicks.

Over the years, Juventus, the legendary Italian club, has featured the best players from around the globe, including Platini, Zidane, and Pirlo, just to name a few. As of 2018, Cristiano Ronaldo joined Juventus after being traded from Real Madrid (though he didn't make an appearance in this particular MLS All-Star Game).

The MLS All-Star Game Fan XI[7] consisted of:

Josef Martinez (Atlanta United)
Miguel Almiron (Atlanta United)

Ezequiel Barco (Atlanta United)
Michael Parkhurst (Atlanta United)
Darlington Nagbe (Atlanta United)*
Brad Guzan (Atlanta United)
Graham Zusi (Sporting Kansas City)
Laurent Ciman (Los Angeles FC)
Carlos Vela (Los Angeles FC)
Diego Valeri (Portland Timbers)
Zlatan Ibrahimovic (LA Galaxy)†

2018 END-OF-SEASON MLS STANDINGS

By the end of September 2018, Atlanta United was atop the Eastern Conference with New York City FC, New York Red Bulls, and Columbus Crew close behind.

As of October 1, 2018, Atlanta United remained in the lead, slightly ahead of the Red Bulls. Here's how it looked in the Eastern Conference:

1 Atlanta United
2 New York Red Bulls
3 New York City FC
4 Columbus Crew
5 Philadelphia Union

---

*   After dealing with an injury, Nagbe did not play in the actual All-Star game.

†   Ibrahimovic did not play in the All-Star game.

6 Montreal Impact
7 D.C. United
8 New England Revolution
9 Toronto FC
10 Chicago Fire
11 Orlando City SC

In the Western Conference, as of late September 2018, Sporting Kansas City, FC Dallas, and Los Angeles FC were in the lead, with Salt Lake, Portland, and Seattle close behind.

As October 1, 2018 came around, the Western Conference looked like this:

1 FC Dallas
2 Sporting Kansas City
3 Los Angeles FC
4 Portland Timbers
5 Seattle Sounders
6 Real Salt Lake
7 LA Galaxy
8 Vancouver Whitecaps
9 Minnesota United
10 Houston Dynamo
11 Colorado Rapids
12 San Jose Earthquakes

As the 2018 season ended there were two big surprises: D.C. United managed to finish in fourth place, qualifying for the playoffs, whereas LA Galaxy finished in seventh place and did not qualify for the playoffs.

By the end of the season, these were the 2018 MLS Standings (teams in bold qualified for the Audi 2018 MLS Cup Playoffs):

Eastern Conference

1 New York Red Bulls
2 Atlanta United FC
3 New York City FC
4 D.C. United
5 Columbus Crew
6 Philadelphia Union
7 Montreal Impact
8 New England Revolution
9 Toronto FC
10 Chicago Fire
11 Orlando City SC

Western Conference

1 Sporting Kansas City
2 Seattle Sounders FC
3 Los Angeles FC
4 FC Dallas
5 Portland Timbers
6 Real Salt Lake
7 LA Galaxy
8 Vancouver Whitecaps FC
9 Houston Dynamo
10 Minnesota United FC
11 Colorado Rapids
12 San Jose Earthquakes

As fall was setting in, things were getting interesting as the 2018 MLS Playoffs were right around the corner.

2018 MLS CUP

The MLS Cup is the coveted league championship, held every year.

AUDI 2018 MLS CUP PLAYOFFS

Eastern Conference

Knockout Round	Conference Semi-Finals	Conference Finals
NYCFC (w) v. Philadelphia Union	NYCFC v. Atlanta United FC (w)	Atlanta United FC (w) v. NY Red Bulls
D.C. United v. Columbus Crew (w)	Columbus Crew v. NY Red Bulls (w)	

*(w) = winner.

Western Conference

Knockout Round	Conference Semi-Finals	Conference Finals
FC Dallas v. Portland Timbers (w)	Portland Timbers (w) v. Seattle Sounders FC	Portland Timbers (w) v. Sporting Kansas City
Los Angeles FC v. Real Salt Lake (w)	Real Salt Lake v. Sporting Kansas City (w)	

*(w) = winner.

MLS Cup
Atlanta United FC (w) v. Portland Timbers

- The Knockout Round was a one-game playoff.
- The Conference Semi-Finals and Conference Finals had two legs (a home and away game).
- The MLS Cup Final had one game. (The team with the most regular-season points hosts the MLS Cup.)

For the real detail-oriented aficionados out there, the following 2018 MLS Playoff Schedule was posted at the MLS website:

AUDI 2018 MLS CUP PLAYOFFS SCHEDULE

This information is subject to change. Canadian and international broadcast information to be announced at a later date.

KNOCKOUT ROUND (October 31 and November 1) Conference third seed vs. sixth seed, and fourth seed vs. fifth seed in a single-game elimination match

Eastern and Western Conference Knockout Round (four games)

- Wednesday, October 31: Times TBD – UniMás, English-Language broadcast TBA
- Wednesday, October 31: Times TBD – UniMás, English-Language broadcast TBA

- Thursday, November 1: Times TBD – UniMás, English-Language broadcast TBA
- Thursday, November 1: Times TBD – UniMás, English-Language broadcast TBA

CONFERENCE SEMIFINALS (November 4 and 11) Two-game series, aggregate-goal, home-and-home format between conference top seed vs. lowest advancing seed from Knockout Round and conference second seed vs. highest seed from Knockout Round

Eastern Conference Semifinal Series: Leg 1 (two games)

- Sunday, November 4: Time TBD – TV to be announced
- Sunday, November 11: Time TBD – TV to be announced

Eastern Conference Semifinal Series: Leg 2 (two games)

- Sunday, November 4: Time TBD – TV to be announced
- Sunday, November 11: Time TBD – TV to be announced

Western Conference Semifinal Series: Leg 1 (two games)

- Sunday, November 4: Time TBD – TV to be announced
- Sunday, November 11: Time TBD – TV to be announced

Western Conference Semifinal Series: Leg 2 (two games)

- Sunday, November 4: Time TBD – TV to be announced
- Sunday, November 11: Time TBD – TV to be announced

CONFERENCE CHAMPIONSHIPS (November 25 and 29)
Two-game series, aggregate-goal, home-and-home format

Eastern Conference Championship: Leg 1

- Sunday, November 25: Time TBD – TV to be announced

Eastern Conference Championship: Leg 2

- Thursday, November 29: Time TBD – TV to be announced

Western Conference Championship: Leg 1

- Sunday, November 25: Time TBD – TV to be announced

Western Conference Championship: Leg 2

- Thursday, November 29: Time TBD – TV to be announced

2018 MLS CUP (December 8)
Hosted at the home venue of the finalist with the best regular
season record

- Saturday, December 8: 7:30 PM ET – FOX, UniMás, TSN,
  TVA Sports[8]

As in previous years it didn't disappoint.

2018 US OPEN CUP

Arguably the second best tournament for MLS teams is the US Open Cup. "The Lamar Hunt US Open Cup, commonly known as the US Open Cup (USOC), is a knock-out cup competition in American soccer. It is the oldest ongoing national soccer competition in the US. The 105th edition, held in 2018, was contested by 97 clubs from the two professional leagues sanctioned by the United States Soccer Federation: Major League Soccer (MLS), and the United Soccer League (USL), along with amateur clubs in the earlier rounds of the tournament after qualifying through their leagues. The overall champion earns a total of $300,000 in prize money, while the runner-up receives $100,000, and the furthest-advancing team from each lower-division league receives $25,000. In addition, the tournament winner qualifies for the group stage of the CONCACAF Champions League.

The competition was first held during the 1913-1914 season as the National Challenge Cup, with Brooklyn Field Club winning a trophy donated by Thomas Dewar for the promotion of American soccer. It was renamed and then dedicated to MLS owner Lamar Hunt by the United States Soccer Federation in 1999."[9]

For the US Open Cup, there are many preliminary games which lead up to the round of 16. From 2018, those rounds are listed below, in which teams from around the country battled it out. These were teams of a lower rank than MLS. (Essentially, the fourth round is where MLS teams make an appearance, taking on teams from lower ranks.)

Instead of listing the myriad of games from these early rounds (which is quite extensive), we skip ahead to the round of 16.

Play-in round
First round
Second round
Third round
Fourth round
Round of 16
Quarterfinals
Semifinals
Final

Round of 16
(Games played during June 2018)

Portland Timbers 1
LA Galaxy 0

Philadelphia Union 2
New York Red Bulls 1

Sporting Kansas City 3
FC Dallas 2

Houston Dynamo 1
Minnesota United FC 0

D.C. United 1
Orlando City SC 1 (won in penalty kicks)

Louisville City FC 2
Nashville SC 1

Atlanta United FC 0
Chicago Fire 1

Los Angeles FC 3
Sacramento Republic FC 2

Quarterfinals
(Games played during July 2018)

Philadelphia Union 1
Orlando City SC 0

Chicago Fire 4
Louisville City FC 0

Houston Dynamo 4
Sporting Kansas City 2

Los Angeles FC 3
Portland Timbers 2

Semifinals
(Games played during August 2018)

Philadelphia Union 3
Chicago Fire 0

Houston Dynamo 3 (won in penalty kicks)
Los Angeles FC 3

Final

(Played on September 26, 2018 at BBVA Compass Stadium, Houston, Texas)

Houston Dynamo 3
Philadelphia Union 0

Houston took home the US Open Cup without much resistance from Philadelphia in a 3-0 victory. Two of those goals came from the star of the game, Mauro Manotas, while the third was an own-goal surrendered by Philadelphia.

Broadcast on ESPN2, it was evident that Houston was going to add another trophy to its case, not a good showing for Philadelphia.

The first half was a lot of Houston, while Philadelphia struggled to find an answer. The second half presented itself as much of the same; however, Philadelphia got some momentum going with sporadic chances, putting Houston on its heels a bit, but they couldn't provide enough magic to get anything going in terms of realistically challenging for the title. It was a good showing for Houston, and this was the first US Open title for the franchise.

2018 SUPPORTERS' SHIELD

Supporters' Shield is pretty straightforward: At the end of each season, the team with the best MLS record wins the Supporters' Shield.

The 2018 winners: New York Red Bulls.

While the Red Bulls had a stellar season, relying on strong defense and the potent scoring threat of Bradley Wright-Phillips, other teams that were knocking on the door of the Supporters' Shield included Atlanta United, LAFC, and Sporting Kansas City.

Atlanta United was arguably the best team in the league with the best style along with the most dynamic offense; it was led by Josef Martinez, the goal-scoring wonder of Venezuela. By season's end, Atlanta's record was close to overtaking the Red Bulls'. Bob Bradley deserves a lot of credit. LAFC (a club dedicated to possession passing) was easily playing one of the best styles of soccer in the league, second only to Atlanta.

Sporting Kansas City was solid all year, with a steady passing game under the coaching leadership of Peter Vermes, along with the experienced on-field presence of Matt Besler and Graham Zusi.

In the Western Conference, Seattle, Dallas, and Portland also had good runs.

2018 CAMPEONES CUP

Toronto FC vs. Tigres UANL
1-3
September 19, 2018
Hosted at BMO Field
Toronto, Canada

Starting lineups
Toronto FC
Alex Bono GK
Eriq Zavaleta D
Michael Bradley D
Nick Hagglund D
Gregory van der Wiel M
Jay Chapman M
Marky Delgado M
Jonathan Osorio M
Justin Morrow M
Jozy Altidore F
Sebastian Giovinco F

Tigres
Nahuel Guzman GK
Luis Rodriguez D
Jesus Duenas D
Hugo Ayala D
Juninho D
Jorge Torres Nilo D
Rafael Carioca M
Guido Pizarro M
Lucas Zelarayan M
Eduardo Vargas F
Andre-Pierre Gignac F

It was the first of its kind, the inaugural Campeones Cup. Essentially, this new cup is played by the previous year's league winners of MLS and Liga MX. Taylor Twellman, the color commentator for ESPN2, was excited about the game's future prospects, pointing out that people might want to check back in a few years' time to see where the event stands. What was at stake? To be the first winner, for starters—that's always nice—and a prize of $100,000. Not bad.

Tigres, sporting yellow-white-yellow uniforms, was stacked with talent, including Gignac (who was with France in the 2010 World Cup) and Vargas (one of Chile's best exports). In the first half Toronto, wearing red uniforms, had selective moments, but, when all was said and done, Tigres had the majority of possession and better play. There was a hopeful moment when Toronto had a header that went off the crossbar, but then its luck got worse when Giovinco (the 2015 MLS MVP) left with an injury. The Mexican side got on the board first to break the silence. A through-ball chipped down the left side led to a near-post goal from Duenas.

The second half was much of the same. While Toronto had some moments, the play was pretty much in the hands of Tigres. Duenas stepped up for his second goal that came off a rebound, and, from outside the box, he put home a low shot in the left corner with pace. The third goal was an own-goal from Toronto's Zavaleta.

Eventually, Toronto received a penalty kick from a handball that was scored by Janson at the end of the game. It was in the books. After playing a very controlled and well-thought-out game, Tigres took home the first Campeones Cup, along with $100,000.

2018 CONCACAF CHAMPIONS LEAGUE

1st Place: Guadalajara (Mexico)

2nd Place: Toronto FC

Toronto's Sebastian Giovinco (the former Juventus man) was named Best Player for the tournament.

2018 KEY PLAYER MOVES

A few key moves in 2018 saw Darlington Nagbe leave the Portland Timbers, packing his bags for Atlanta. Felipe of Brazil switched from New York Red Bulls to Vancouver Whitecaps. Zlatan Ibrahimovic, who was with Manchester United, joined LA Galaxy. Wayne Rooney left Everton for D.C. United. Speaking of Wayne Rooney, as *USA Today* wrote, he joined "David Beckham (Los Angeles Galaxy), Frank Lampard (New York City FC), Steven Gerrard (LA Galaxy) and Ashley Cole (LA Galaxy) as former England national team stars who made the move to MLS."[10]

The good news with foreign signings is that MLS is still a place for top talent to land. This is evidenced by so many star players ending up in America. This helps with expansion. And that's what the league wants and needs in order to grow and to become the world's next super league.

MLS EXPANSION

Expansion is on the move in MLS, so much so that it seems to be the theme of the league, with drumbeats calling for more.

From a piece in *The Washington Post*, Norman Chad summed this up, saying that "as recently as 2004, there were only 10 MLS franchises. At the moment, there are 23, with plans for 26 by 2020 or so and 28 soon thereafter. Like Starbucks, there soon will be an MLS franchise on every city corner. The expansion has come fast, furious, and curious. In 2015, teams were added in New York and Orlando; in 2017, in Atlanta and Minnesota; and in 2018, in Los Angeles. Nashville and Miami are the next expansion sites, with Cincinnati, Detroit, and Sacramento competing to become MLS's 26th franchise."[11]

CINCINNATI, OHIO

FC Cincinnati will field a team in the 2019 MLS season. Ohio, a passionate soccer state, will get their second MLS team. With that said, in 2018, there was talk of Columbus possibly moving elsewhere, which—if such a thing happened—would be terrible for the in-state rivalry between Columbus and Cincinnati. As things stand, two Ohio teams will compete in MLS, adding much depth to the league. For Cincinnati, it will be another pro team for their city, along with the Bengals and Reds.

MIAMI, FLORIDA

As of July 2018, David Beckham and Jorge Mas—who joined together as owners of the MLS expansion team in Miami—were in the midst of building a stadium. Each year, the rent and taxes for the land will cost around $44 million, according to mlssoccer. com[12] (accessed on July 9, 2018). At one time, Miami had an MLS team, the Miami Fusion, which featured Roy Lassiter,

Jay Heaps, Chris Henderson, Preki, Carlos Valderrama, Eric Wynalda, and others; it eventually folded, and the city is hoping this time around it will be permanent.

NASHVILLE, TENNESSEE

Country music's capital will be getting a soccer team. Nashville's first MLS season should be in 2020. Professional soccer is right around the corner; planning is underway in Tennessee. The formation of a team—from its conception to the actual 11-player lineup standing on a field—is usually an adventure that spans the course of a few years, if not more.

In December of 2017, a story from the official MLS website (www.mlssoccer.com), written by Nick Rosano, laid out some of the details: "Nashville's MLS team will be owned by the investment group, Nashville Soccer Holdings, LLC, led by John R. Ingram, the chairman of Ingram Industries Inc. Ingram's partners in the soccer club include Minnesota Vikings owners Mark, Zygi, and Leonard Wilf, and the Turner Family, managing partners of Nashville-based MarketStreet Enterprises. As a result of a private-public partnership between the club's owners and the community, the team will play in a new, 27,500-seat soccer stadium at The Fairgrounds Nashville in the capital city's artistic Wedgewood-Houston neighborhood."[13]

In January of 2018, *The Wall Street Journal* featured the ongoing process with a piece by Justin Owen: "A few weeks ago, Major League Soccer announced it was headed to Nashville, Tennessee. The league should thank local taxpayers, who will fork over millions to help build a new $275 million stadium for the expansion franchise."[14] That's one way to get a stadium built. Proponents of Nashville receiving an MLS franchise would likely argue that it will bring jobs to the community, which would in turn be good for the local economy.

BUDGETS 2018

The following player salary information was provided by Daniel Boniface and Joe Nguyen at *The Denver Post* on May 10, 2018, and updated on July 11, 2018.

Top 10 highest-paid players in MLS in 2018[15]

Player	Team	Position	Base Salary	Compensation
Sebastian Giovinco	Toronto FC	F	$5,600,000.00	$7,115,555.67
Michael Bradley	Toronto FC	M	$6,000,000.00	$6,500,000.00
Carlos Vela	LAFC	F	$4,500,000.00	$6,292,500.00
Bastian Schweinsteiger	Chicago Fire	M	$6,100,000.08	$6,100,000.08
Giovani dos Santos	LA Galaxy	F	$4,250,000.00	$6,000,000.00
David Villa	New York City FC	F	$5,610,000.00	$5,610,000.00
Jozy Altidore	Toronto FC	F	$5,000,000.00	$5,000,000.00
Ignacio Piatti	Montreal Impact	M	$500,000.04	$4,713,333.37
Tim Howard	Colorado Rapids	GK	$2,000,000.00	$2,475,000.00
Diego Valeri	Portland Timbers	M	$2,320,000.00	$2,380,000.00

As you can see, Toronto FC leads the list.

Following is a snippet of budget activity from MLS, released in 2018.

2018 MLS Roster Composition

A Major League Soccer club's active roster may have up to 30 players. All 30 players are eligible for selection to each 18-player game-day squad during the regular season and playoffs.

In addition to the salary budget, each MLS club spends additional funds on player compensation, including money from a league-wide allocation pool (general and targeted allocation money), the cost of designated players outside the salary budget, and money spent on the supplemental and reserve rosters (roster spots 21-30).

On-Budget: Senior Roster

Up to 20 players, occupying roster spots 1-20, count against the club's 2018 salary budget of US$4,035,000, and are referred to collectively as the club's senior roster.

- Roster spots 19 and 20 are not required to be filled, and teams may spread their salary budget across only 18 salary budget players. A minimum salary budget charge will be imputed against a team's salary budget for each unfilled senior roster spot below 18.
- A club may have no more than twenty players on its senior roster, subject to the season-ending injury replacement, disabled list, and loan exceptions.

- The maximum budget charge for a single player is US$504,375.

Off-Budget: Supplemental and Reserve Rosters

The salaries of players on the supplemental roster (spots 21-24) and reserve roster (spots 25-30) do not count toward a club's salary budget.

Supplemental Roster

Players occupying roster spots 21-24 do not count against the club's salary budget, and are referred to collectively as the club's supplemental roster. A club may have no more than four players on its supplemental roster, subject to the season-ending injury replacement, disabled list, and loan exceptions.

- Slots 21-24 may be filled with (i) senior minimum salary budget charge payers (US$67,500 in 2018) which may include homegrown players, (ii) Generation adidas players, or (iii) any specifically designated players eligible for the MLS SuperDraft; or (iv) homegrown players earning more than the senior minimum salary subject to the homegrown player subsidy.
- All Generation adidas players are supplemental roster players until they graduate from the program.
- All players on the supplemental roster must be paid a base salary that is at least the senior minimum salary (US$67,500).

Reserve Roster

- Players occupying roster slots 25-28 may be filled with players earning either (i) the reserve minimum salary (US$54,500 in 2018) or (ii) homegrown players earning more than the reserve minimum salary subject to the homegrown player subsidy.
- Reserve minimum salary players must be 24 years or younger during the league year (age of player is determined by year—not date—of birth).
- These slots may not be filled with senior minimum salary players or Generation adidas players.
- All players in slots 25-28 must be paid a base salary that is at least the reserve minimum salary (US$54,500).

Reserve Roster spots 29 and 30

- Players occupying roster spots 29 and 30 must be homegrown players and will follow the same roster and budget rules as homegrown players occupying reserve roster spots 25-28.

Treatment of Homegrown Players on a Club's Roster

If a homegrown player is initially added to a club's supplemental or reserve roster and subsequently moved to the senior roster, they may only be moved back to the supplemental or reserve roster if they are earning either (i) the senior minimum salary or (ii) reserve minimum salary.

Homegrown Player Subsidy

- Homegrown player(s) in roster slots 21-30 may earn in aggregate each year up to $125,000 above the reserve minimum salary (if occupying spots 25-30) or senior minimum salary (if occupying spots 21-24).
- Clubs may use up to $200,000 of their currently available targeted allocation money (i.e., amounts awarded through 2018) to sign new homegrown players to their first MLS contract, subject to league review and approval. Targeted allocation money cannot be used on a homegrown player previously signed to MLS.[16]

THE MLS TEAMS 2019

Eastern Conference

Atlanta United FC
Chicago Fire
Columbus Crew SC
D.C. United
Montreal Impact
New England Revolution
New York City FC
New York Red Bulls
Orlando City SC
Philadelphia Union
Toronto FC

Western Conference

Colorado Rapids
FC Dallas
Houston Dynamo
LA Galaxy
Los Angeles FC
Minnesota United FC
Portland Timbers

Real Salt Lake
San Jose Earthquakes
Seattle Sounders FC
Sporting Kansas City
Vancouver Whitecaps FC

A few expansion teams that have been in the works include Miami, Cincinnati, and Nashville.

Teams that have folded include Chivas USA (2005-2014), Miami Fusion (1998-2001), and the Tampa Bay Mutiny (1996-2001).

The MLS Season: March to October

MAJOR LEAGUE SOCCER

An In-Depth Look at the Teams[*]

---

[*]   Trades may have occurred after the publication of this book.

ATLANTA UNITED FC

Twitter: @ATLUTD
First season: 2017
MLS Cup: 1
US Open Cup: 0
Supporters' Shield: 0

Known For
Strong attendance
Very passionate fans
Exciting games
Arthur Blank
Darlington Nagbe
Josef Martinez
Miguel Almiron
Hector Villalba
Ezequiel Barco
Michael Parkhurst
Brad Guzan

A BRIEF TEAM HISTORY

In only its second year, Atlanta United FC won the 2018 MLS
Cup at home in front of over 70,000 fans after defeating Portland

2-0. Atlanta United FC is a team that is currently sweeping MLS off its feet with excitement, pure offense, and goals left and right.

Atlanta came into existence as an expansion team in 2014, playing its first MLS game in 2017 (a late start to MLS for sure). However, during the 2017 season, the team had a good result, placing fourth in the Eastern Conference. The team plays its games at Mercedes-Benz Stadium, with a capacity of 42,500, with room for expansion to approximately 70,000.

Arthur Blank—who co-founded Home Depot, owns the Atlanta Falcons and Atlanta United FC, and has a net worth of around $3 billion—has overseen the development of United FC in an area passionate for soccer. When thinking of soccer in the US, Georgia may not come to mind right away, but it's a state that has produced many good players, including Clint Mathis and Josh Wolff. It's a region with a strong fan base who are excited about their new team and ready to win.

In 2016, Gerardo Martino—who was born in Argentina, and who played one game for his country's national team as a midfielder in 1991—was hired as the coach.

Team president Darren Eales—who was born in England— is part of the equation moving forward, and the goal is to take Atlanta straight to the top of the league. In doing so, it has tough competition in its conference, with teams like New York City FC, the Columbus Crew, and the New York Red Bulls coming off a good year in 2018. For a team founded in 2014 and that played its first MLS game in 2017, Atlanta is moving forward quickly and in a good direction. From an article in 2018, Andrew Das of *The New York Times* wrote that "Atlanta United broke attendance records in its inaugural season and then broke the bank this winter, signing the Argentine teenager Ezequiel Barco for a fee reported to be $15 million."[17] Furthermore, talk about an incredible season for Josef Martinez, who made MLS history for hat tricks and surpassed the single-season scoring record; he also won the league MVP award.

In 2018, there was a buzz surrounding Atlanta that has rarely occurred in the history of American soccer. Whether you were an avid fan or someone that tuned in from time to time, it was nearly impossible to avoid hearing about the soccer storm brewing in Atlanta. Some home games brought in over 70,000 fans who were revved up, like the Coliseum of ancient Rome, anxiously anticipating the next goal and exploding with ecstasy when the ball crashed into the back of the net. Wherever Atlanta played, excitement was around the corner.

When Tiger Woods was in his prime, people would change their schedule just to watch him on TV. For American soccer fans, that was Atlanta United during 2018. As Tiger Woods made an uncool sport like golf cool, Atlanta United made soccer a whole lot cooler as well.

As Atlanta navigates 2019, it's looking to cash in on attendance, goals, and excitement—all of which it's providing plenty of so far.

US OPEN CUP

To date, Atlanta United has not won a US Open Cup.

FACTS ABOUT THEIR CITY

Atlanta—the land of Southern cooking; Coca-Cola; and the Braves, Hawks, and Falcons, along with a little music—has a population of around 400,000-500,000, with around 5.7 million people in the greater metro area. There are a lot of passionate sports fans in Atlanta with soccer rising toward the top of the list.

Atlanta-style parties will be in full swing around game time, as many locals enjoy a wide selection of domestic beer available from Southern Beer Tours, Atlanta Brews Cruise, Monday Night Brewing, and Second Self Beer Company. The Atlanta United supporters' groups—The Faction, Footie Mob, Resurgence, and Terminus Legion—are ready to party.

WHERE THE TEAM IS TODAY: TACTICS AND STRATEGIES

Offensively, in 2018, Atlanta fielded a number of Argentinian players, who, alongside Nagbe, combined to make a strong passing build-up. While Nagbe was injured for a large part of the season, the team stepped up and continued to dominate possession against opponents. Julian Gressel was usually found out wide where he served up many assists throughout the year. The remainder of the attack mainly consisted of Miguel Almiron, Ezequiel Barco, Hector Villalba, and the man with a plan—to score, that is—Josef Martinez. Many times the offensive potency of Atlanta completely overwhelmed confused defenses.

Brad Guzan—the talented keeper from Evergreen Park, Illinois— has the luxury of watching one of the most fine-tuned defensive backfields in the league. Part of Atlanta's defensive success arises from its technical ability on the ball, which, in turn, gives its actual defensive responsibilities a cushion. Essentially, all of Atlanta's time on the ball causes its opponents to become flustered once they eventually do gain possession, and thus their attack is predictable, rushed, and futile. This plays right into the hands—or feet—of Atlanta's defense. Atlanta is one of the few teams in the league that employs a firm defense that kickstarts a thoughtful and vibrant attack. It achieves this with swift yet patient passing from the backline defenders, who often control the point of attack with a thoughtful possession-oriented approach. As a result, much of its success as a team lies rooted in the passing ability of the backline. Such players featured in the 2018 campaign include Franco Escobar, Michael Parkhurst, Leandro Gonzalez Pirez, Chris McCann, with Jeff Larentowicz operating as a go-between defensive midfielder.

Don't be surprised to see a 4-2-3-1 or 4-1-4-1 formation, with Martinez up top, or perhaps a 3-4-1-2, with Martinez paired up top with another forward.

FRANK DE BOER: A BRIEF COACHING PORTRAIT

Gerardo Martino—born in 1962—accepted the Atlanta United coaching position in 2016, and his team jumped into the 2017 season. As of 2018, there were a number of South American players on the team, with a handful from Argentina, Martino's home country. As a player, he made one appearance with Argentina. He has coached a number of teams, including the national sides of Paraguay and Argentina.

Under Martino's guidance, Atlanta played with a fluid style, often dominating possession while creating many scoring chances. In many respects, Martino deserves a ton of credit for Atlanta's early success. After all, he led the team to its first MLS Cup championship. He left to accept another coaching position, speculated to be Mexico.

The new coach, Frank de Boer, a former Dutch national team star, will have a lot to live up to; at the same time, he has an incredibly talented group, one that has great potential to repeat as MLS champions.

KEY PLAYERS AND THEIR CHARACTERISTICS

Darlington Nagbe, Josef Martinez, and Hector Villalba

In 2018, Atlanta United made a major acquisition by getting Darlington Nagbe, a true passing genius. (Portland's loss is Atlanta's gain.) With the guidance of coach Caleb Porter, Nagbe won the MLS Cup with the Timbers, and he looks to bring this experience to the table for Atlanta. As a rising star and leader in midfield with the USMNT, Nagbe is a great asset for any team, and Atlanta is lucky to have him on the field. It is possible that, when all is said and done, Nagbe will be the best midfielder the USMNT has ever had. He brings detail-oriented passing to the possession game, which is extremely hard to teach; and he has a special quality in the midfield that brings teammates together, stringing passes with great accuracy and rhythm, as if Xavi and Beckenbauer were telepathically guiding him along. If he continues to be surrounded by like-minded passing-first players with an eye for good possession, Nagbe should bring the fans of Atlanta United much happiness in the immediate future.

Josef Martinez—born in Venezuela—is a talented scoring threat for Atlanta, now known as the scoring king of MLS; we'll get to that in a second. He's also known as the 2018 MLS MVP. He's a forward with over 35 games with Venezuela since his debut in 2011. But he's not so much known for his remarkable talents with Venezuela, a country eager to make a name for itself on the World Cup stage someday; and that day may come soon with Martinez around.

Since the 2017 MLS season, Martinez has already slotted in a record number of goals for Atlanta, taking the Eastern Conference of MLS by storm. The 2018 MLS season was monumental for Martinez. In July, in a game against D.C. United, he made headlines around the country. *USA Today* reported that Josef Martinez had "set an MLS record with his sixth career hat trick and Atlanta United rallied to beat D.C. United 3-1 on Saturday."[18] From that victory over D.C. United, Martinez was still on the move, looking for more, anticipating the next game.

Then, just like that, another record was waiting on the door step. During the 2018 MLS campaign, Martinez was slotting in so many goals that he began edging closer and closer to the all-time single-season scoring record of 27, set by Roy Lassiter in 1996, and tied by Chris Wondolowski in 2012 and Bradley

Wright-Phillips in 2014. For some reason, 27 was the magic number; no one could get past it. Then on August 24, 2018, on the road against Orlando City SC, Martinez scored his 28th goal of the year, breaking the all-time record and becoming the MLS king of goals. Aside from that record-breaking goal, however, he didn't receive as many touches as he should have.

Orlando's defense—led in the back by former Manchester United member Jonathan Spector, with his supporting cast of teammates wearing purple uniforms—was holding up fairly well. There was a feeling of consternation, that maybe it wouldn't happen on this night; after all, leading into this game, any announcer worth his weight in gold predicted that, not only would he break the record, he would annihilate it. So the feeling was: *Let's do it already!*

Atlanta—wearing all-white uniforms with orange trim—was passing the ball beautifully, as usual. Then, around the 74th minute, it all came together. Martinez didn't just break the record with a tap-in or penalty kick. Not even close. He received a pass around the top of the box, then dribbled past a player with his left foot, and then, with his right foot, calmly chipped the ball over the keeper. Brilliant. Pure class. That's when Martinez—who's built a little like Roy Lassiter, wears his socks halfway down the shin, is muscular like a gymnast, and has blond streaks in his hair (styled in a miniature mohawk, of course)—took off his shirt, and held it up, ostensibly to the fans, while he both passionately and nonchalantly embraced the epic moment. His teammates had gathered around, cameras were clicking, the Atlanta fans in the stands were cheering, and the announcers, along with scores of fans watching the game on ESPN, were in awe. Later that night, the monumental goal—which, by the way, happened to be the game winner in a 2-1 victory over Orlando City

SC—was replayed on SportsCenter with Scott Van Pelt. History was made that night, and he wasn't done. By season's end, Martinez eventually tallied an amazing 31 goals. (Note: The MLS does not count goals scored during the 2018 MLS Cup Playoffs.)

This is exactly what Atlanta fans should want on the field. Martinez—whose play comes across like a mix between Romario and Roy Lassiter—is not a major aerial threat, which is a benefit; he leans more toward an attack around goal with skill and guile where his speed and quickness can be put to good use, getting exceptional results over the long run, as opposed to crossing the ball into the box for headers. With Nagbe, Barco, and Gressel* distributing smart passes from the midfield, this should be a lethal combination for any opponent to deal with. As a result, Martinez, the returning 2018 MLS MVP, will be high on the list of concerns for any defense.

Hector Villalba—the youngster from Argentina, born in 1994— is a quick player that brings a lot of energy to Atlanta's offense. Speed, elusive moves, and a strong shot, along with a crafty touch around goal are just a few of the assets he brings to his team.

---

*   The list of talented passers on Atlanta United seems to go on, ad infinitum.

KEY PLAYER STATS

(Total career goals with this club)

	Games Played	Goals	Scoring Percentage
Darlington Nagbe	28	1	3%
Josef Martinez	57	55	96%
Hector Villalba	62	20	32%

WHAT TO WATCH FOR ON TV: HOW BRADLEY, IBRAHIMOVIC, NAGBE, AND OTHERS PLAY

The high-flying, fluid, skillful team known as Atlanta United FC overwhelmed the 2018 MLS All-Star Game with players, and their top player, Josef Martinez, won the All-Star Game MVP award, whose ownership group is likely high-fiving so much they need wrist braces. This is a group of super-talented guys currently taking the league by storm, producing clinic after clinic of how to score goals. They're simply an offensive force of nature. How is Atlanta accomplishing such a thing? For one, they have the passing wisdom of Nagbe in the midfield, and he's surrounded with offensive talent (including Ezequiel Barco), not defensive, safe-playing, steady, boring players that keep games close.

If anything can be learned from Spain (2008-2012), it's that offensive players (who would ordinarily be thought of as weak individual defensive players) are perfect defenders because if they control the game with possession, then theoretically it's always easy to retain the ball (because the opposing team, once they attain possession of the ball, is so overwhelmed with not previously having it that they end up acting erratically, trying to do too much, forcing things, and eventually turning the ball over). Atlanta falls into this category, reflecting aspects of Spain's approach.

Atlanta is also a team that is predominately under six feet tall. In my book, *Why American Soccer Isn't There Yet,* I explain that a tactic like this (i.e., using players under six feet tall, as opposed to taller players) is beneficial for a team's success in the modern era. As a result, Atlanta is not relying on an aerial attack, instead seeking to swarm its opponents with skillful interplay, which is always more advantageous in soccer (over the course of a season, or in an extended tournament like the World Cup).

Free kicks tend to go in favor of Jeff Larentowicz, who, in 2018, ranked second of all time in MLS for goals made from free kicks, behind the leader, Sebastian Giovinco, in Toronto. Generally speaking, if Larentowicz is shooting, stay out of the way—he has an absolute cannon.

Michael Parkhurst won't be accused of being Usain Bolt, even by his own teammates, but he makes up for it with good anticipation. He's also a defender with experience on the USMNT, so, along with his background, the steady hand of Brad Guzan in goal, and the offensive talent up front, Atlanta United is stacked with talent and sure to be a contender.

Amazing Atlanta won its first MLS Cup in only two MLS seasons. It did so on December 8, 2018 in front of over 70,000 fans at home by defeating Portland 2-0. Arthur Blank, the owner, who also owns the Atlanta Falcons, couldn't have done a better job constructing this team of remarkable players and the dream season that just finished up (a season in which Atlanta almost captured the Supporters' Shield). Arguably, this will go down as an all-time great MLS team, and probably the best to date, notwithstanding D.C. United of the late 90s which had a very talented squad. Not to go into too much detail regarding other dominant MLS clubs of yore, it should be known that very few of them can boast playing the game as well as Atlanta did in 2018. The style it exuded was top notch. As I predicted on October 22, 2018, Atlanta United would win the 2018 MLS Cup. One reason for the prediction was Atlanta's playing style. Going into the nuances of such a thing would take many paragraphs, pages, and, well, frankly, a book, but know this: To play with a top-notch style is not easily done or even understood by most. Though, when it's accomplished, it should very likely bring long-term success, such was the case with Barcelona and Spain during the Golden Generation. Atlanta is currently tapping into that area of brilliance; however, things may be unraveling as we speak. Its coach, the great Gerardo Martino, moved on to coaching Mexico while it was announced during the 2018 MLS Cup final that Miguel Almiron would be heading to Europe. (This could be a problem because Almiron and Nagbe, separately, are elegant passers, and, together, they were a lethal combination that provided great flow to the offense. Almiron's departure is like breaking up Xavi and Iniesta. Nagbe will have to find further passing outlets with Barco and others.) Despite these changes, should Parkhurst, Nagbe, Martinez, Barco, and others stay around, the chances of a repeat should be good. The 2019 MLS season for Atlanta will be a very interesting one, to say the least.

Will it take 36 years for Atlanta to win the MLS Cup again? Considering its fast start, a gambling man would probably say no. Should Atlanta's lineup stay together, and remain injury-free, this is a team that could find itself in multiple finals for the next few years.

Overall Team Rating: 9.8

CHICAGO FIRE

Twitter: @ChicagoFire
First season: 1998
MLS Cup: 1
US Open Cup: 4
Supporters' Shield: 1

Known For
Winning the MLS Cup
Dedicated fans
Rowdy fans that have taken over a section of the stadium[19]
Bob Bradley
Piotr Nowak
Frank Klopas
Ante Razov
Bastian Schweinsteiger

A BRIEF TEAM HISTORY

Chicago Fire—a team with a magnificent history—won the MLS Cup in 1998, which, to date, has been the only time they lifted the trophy. In the Western Conference playoffs, they defeated Colorado, then LA Galaxy before taking down D.C. United in the final game by a score of 2-0. Bob Bradley, who coached the team to victory, won Coach of the Year. At the close of a great season, Bradley's players won major awards; Lubos Kubik won Defender of the Year, and Zach Thornton won Goalkeeper of the Year. Following their championship run, Chicago Fire had a couple second place finishes in the MLS Cup, in 2000 and 2003.

As a soccer franchise in a major sports market, Chicago Fire has a strong fan base, a cornerstone of keeping a franchise in the black. The fans are soccer smart, and the aspiration of getting back to the championship game, and hoisting the trophy once again, looms large every season.

Chicago Fire did well in 2017, placing third in the Eastern Conference. Though, 2018 was a different story as Chicago wound up in 10th place, just above the worst team from the east, Orlando City. Now, as things stand, they're a club eager to get back on top.

US OPEN CUP

Chicago Fire won the US Open Cup in 1998, 2000, 2003, and 2006.

FACTS ABOUT THEIR CITY

Chicago—the city by the lake and home of the White Sox, Cubs, Blackhawks, Bears, Bulls, and Fire—has a population of around 9.5 million people in the greater metro area. A few of the Chicago

Fire supporters' groups ready to get loud are Section 8 Chicago, Fire Ultras, and Sector Latino.

Beer. Chicago has it. It seems like every street corner you walk past has another great must-visit bar, and when it comes to soccer, The Globe Pub—located at 1934 West Irving Park Road—has established itself as the best bar in the city to view soccer games.

WHERE THE TEAM IS TODAY: TACTICS AND STRATEGIES

Some people are of the mindset that offense and defense coalesce into one, that it's all part of the same ongoing process of parts working together in different areas of the field. How can this really be argued with? Perhaps in rec soccer, defenders are defenders, who stand in one place, and forwards are forwards, who also stand in one place. With that said, Chicago had a few players to disperse around the field. In the 2018 season, offensively speaking, the Fire featured Nemanja Nikolic, Luis Solignac, Diego Campos, Raheem Edwards, Alan Gordon, and Aleksandar Katai, along with Drew Conner in midfield and with the versatility and organizational skill of Dax McCarty.

Defensively, a few players in the back included Johan Kappelhof, and Brandon Vincent, with an option of Grant Lillard, while Jorge Corrales and Nicolas Hasler appeared to have defensive and midfield responsibilities out wide. Bastian Schweinsteiger also played a versatile role as a defender and midfielder, while Richard Sanchez tended goal.

Last year's season proved to be a tough one for the Fire. When there are more Ls than Ws, trades can be made, and the formation can be re-examined. In August, during a wave of losses, defender Kevin Ellis was let go, along with midfielder Tony Tchani.

The Fire tinkered with a few different formations, including a 3-4-1-2, a 3-4-2-1, and a 4-2-3-1.

In a *Chicago Tribune* piece from May 2018, John Kass pointed out that what the Chicago Fire fans "need now are a quality winger with speed and a quality attacking midfielder who's in the prime of his career, not ending it."[20] In hindsight, given the losing record the Fire had in 2018, such a wish list made a lot of sense.

There's talk of a new United Soccer League team arriving in Chicago, yet Fire fans are yearning for a better product on the field now. Whether or not that will come about in 2019 is yet to be seen. The Fire has talented players, a tradition of past success, and a whole new year to start over. It's a long season, and much can happen before October, when the Fire hope to be sitting in playoff contention.

VELJKO PAUNOVIC: A BRIEF COACHING PORTRAIT

Veljko Paunovic took over the coaching position for Chicago Fire in 2015. Born in 1977, he played with the national team of Serbia and Montenegro, along with a ton of professional teams, including Philadelphia Union.

Don't be surprised to see a 3-4-1-2 or 3-4-2-1 or perhaps a 4-2-3-1. Because 2018 was not a great year for Paunovic and Chicago Fire, potential tactical changes must be on the minds of the staff moving forward with the 2019 season.

KEY PLAYERS AND THEIR CHARACTERISTICS

Bastian Schweinsteiger, Drew Conner, Dax McCarty, and Grant Lillard

Bastian Schweinsteiger—former Bayern Munich standout, German center midfielder, and World Cup champion—joined Chicago Fire in 2017. After a long run with Bayern Munich (2002-2015), he landed at Manchester United for a spell, where he played 18 games, before eventually making the switch to Chicago.

Like most German players, he's very technically sound, and he brings a great deal of wisdom to each pass delivered. Of late, Schweinsteiger has been relegated to more of a defensive role with Chicago. In almost any case, there should be a well-organized game with Schweinsteiger on the field.

Drew Conner is from the Chicago area and began playing with the Fire in 2016. Keep an eye out for Conner, a player with potential, and one the Fire might look to utilize in midfield more often down the road.

Dax McCarty is a talented midfielder with an eye for connecting passes, which he does very well. He's a practical, possession-oriented thinker on the field. He brings a great deal of experience from New York Red Bulls, as well as a few caps from the USMNT. Watch for McCarty to keep the game flowing with accurate passes.

Grant Lillard is a defender from Illinois brought to the Fire on the Homegrown Player Rule. He's young, and has only gotten started with the team, but the hope is to guide him through the system for a lot of future success.

KEY PLAYER STATS

(Total career goals with this club)

	Games Played	Goals	Scoring Percentage
Bastian Schweinsteiger	55	7	12%
Drew Conner	32	0	0%
Dax McCarty	54	0	0%
Grant Lillard	8	0	0%

WHAT TO WATCH FOR ON TV: HOW BRADLEY, IBRAHIMOVIC, NAGBE, AND OTHERS PLAY

In Chicago, where sports rule, there are many expectations for the Fire to succeed and bring home another trophy. Whether the stadium is in Bridgeview or some other place in the greater Chicago area, the fans support the team with great excitement and commitment, and the team is always ready to provide a good game for the fans. Having said that, the team didn't have the best of years in 2018. Chicago fans can only hold onto the late 90s for so long. They want results. They want a team that can at least be in the middle of the pack.

If 2018 was a firm indication of things to come, expect to see a do-over with the possible return of Johan Kappelhof, Aleksandar Katai, Drew Conner, Raheem Edwards, Dax McCarty, Brandon Vincent, Diego Campos, Nemanja Nikolic, Alan Gordon, Grant Lillard (a former Indiana Hoosier), and Richard Sanchez in goal. As bad as things were last season, expect to see many changes throughout 2019.

Overall Team Rating: 7.1

COLUMBUS CREW SC

Twitter: @ColumbusCrewSC
First season: 1996
MLS Cup: 1
US Open Cup: 1
Supporters' Shield: 3

Known For
Winning the MLS Cup
One of the original 10 MLS teams
Lively games
Very passionate and dedicated fans
Todd Yeagley
Brian Maisonneuve
Frankie Hejduk
Brian McBride
Zack Steffen
Wil Trapp
Gyasi Zardes

A BRIEF TEAM HISTORY

The great Columbus Crew was part of the original MLS lineup back in 1996. It's a team rich with history and a few trophies, along with many great players that have walked through the halls.

The Crew currently plays its games at Mapfre Stadium, which holds about 20,000 people. The team originally played in the Buckeyes' stadium, which holds a capacity of just over 100,000, but it was clear the Crew would need a soccer-specific stadium, which eventually came to fruition.

Columbus is one of those great soccer cities in the US. Many USMNT games have been held in Columbus, with a few classic showdowns against the boys from Mexico, including an exciting 2-0 US victory led by Josh Wolff and Clint Mathis from Georgia. The passion that Columbus fans have brought to the USMNT games spills over to Crew games, and the Crew have consistently been a good team over the years.

Brian McBride leads the team for goals scored (79), and the team has signed many good players over the years, including McBride, Mike Clark, Todd Yeagley, Brian Maisonneuve, and Frankie Hejduk, to name a few.

In 2008, the Crew took home its one and only MLS Cup to date.

US OPEN CUP

Columbus Crew has one US Open Cup title from 2002.

FACTS ABOUT THEIR CITY

Columbus has a population of around 2 million people in the greater metro area. It's the home of Ohio State football and some interesting local breweries, including Lineage Brewing, Seventh Son Brewing Co., and North High Brewing.

There are many awesome, family-friendly restaurants around Columbus, including Milestone 229 and The Pearl. If you get a chance to drop by The Thurman Café, try the Terminator hamburger, which is approximately five pounds, which is a meal some opposing fans enjoy ordering.

Crew Supporters' Union, Hudson Street Hooligans, and La Turbina Amarilla are supporters' groups making noise for Crew games.

WHERE THE TEAM IS TODAY: TACTICS AND STRATEGIES

Operating out of a 4-2-3-1, the Crew found offensive success in 2018 with Pedro Santos, Federico Higuain, Edward Opoku, Artur, and Gyasi Zardes up front, along with the versatile Wil Trapp guiding things from midfield.

Defensively, goalkeeper Zack Steffen had help from Hector Jimenez, Lalas Abubakar, Milton Valenzuela, Gaston Sauro, Jonathan Mensah, and Harrison Afful.

It was a team that played with heart late in games, and it was also a team that had ups and downs throughout the season. One such example comes from a 2018 game against the Red Bulls. Andrew Erickson of *The Columbus Dispatch* wrote that "sloppiness out of the back led to several turnovers that gave the Red Bulls the ball in the final third. The Crew, meanwhile, failed to register a shot in the opening 15 minutes of the second half after logging six on target in the first half."[21] All part of the journey, but unfortunately, the journey did not end with the Crew holding the MLS Cup high in the air. Overall, however, the Crew had a good 2018 season. As 2019 rolls on, watch for attention to detail in each game plan, as the Crew is a team eager to surge to number one.

GREGG BERHALTER (PREVIOUS COACH): A BRIEF COACHING PORTRAIT

As the previous coach for the Crew, Gregg Berhalter had a good 2018 season, pushing his squad forward with a 4-2-3-1 formation and a heavy dose of his Dutch influences.

As 2018 went on, there was a lot of speculation that perhaps Berhalter would be next in line for the USMNT head coaching position. Eventually, in December of 2018, he was hired as coach of the USMNT. Josh Wolff took over as coach for Crew. Wolff, the former forward with USMNT, has a lot to look forward to with Crew, but he also faces a big challenge in keeping the team in top form.

KEY PLAYERS AND THEIR CHARACTERISTICS

Zack Steffen, Ricardo Clark, Gyasi Zardes, and Wil Trapp

Zack Steffen is a goalie that keeps the net safe for the Crew. The Pennsylvania native has been gaining valuable experience with the USMNT and the Crew has a solid performer guarding its goal.

Ricardo Clark is an experienced player that enjoyed a long duration with the USMNT and now, as he's getting older, he's landed with the Crew after many years with Houston. Should he remain with the Crew, Clark is a midfielder known for his defensive ability that can help his side with stability. Along with that, his experience is an additional bonus to help push Columbus forward in a positive direction. However, now that he's in his mid-thirties it will be interesting to see if the Crew hold onto him for much longer; it could be a situation where he's traded at any minute.

Gyasi Zardes—the guy with the yellow mohawk—is a player that has spent some time on the USMNT, but with a change in coaching, his days at that level may be numbered. Whether that's the case or not, he does have experience from that level which should increase his chances of success at Columbus. He also spent many years with the Galaxy, a high-level team that provided him a platform to gain confidence. He has a presence on the wing, and with the right players around him, good things can potentially happen when he's on the ball. Given his experience with the national team and LA Galaxy, he's a player that adds value in a potential trade and because of this he might leave Columbus at any given time.

Wil Trapp has turned into a veteran player for the Crew with over 150 appearances. Trapp earned the AT&T Goal of the Week in July of 2018. On the MLS website, Dylan Butler wrote that "for Wil Trapp, his goals are more about quality than quantity."[22] The midfielder is also making a name for himself with the USMNT.

KEY PLAYER STATS

(Total career goals with this club)

	Games Played	Goals	Scoring Percentage
Zack Steffen	63	0	0%
Ricardo Clark	13	1	7%
Gyasi Zardes	33	19	57%
Wil Trapp	157	2	1%

WHAT TO WATCH FOR ON TV: HOW BRADLEY, IBRAHIMOVIC, NAGBE, AND OTHERS PLAY

What to watch for? Watch to see if the Crew are even a team. Outside of the strong effort in place to relocate the club to Austin, Texas, the Crew has some salient qualities on its side. Watch for solid contributions from Pedro Santos, Federico Higuain, Edward Opoku, Artur, Hector Jimenez, Lalas Abubakar, Milton Valenzuela, Gaston Sauro, Jonathan Mensah, and Harrison Afful. It will be interesting to see if these featured players stay around, given that it's a team in limbo. The question is: Given its uncertain future in Columbus, how does the line-up fluctuate during such a time? It may or may not. One thing's for certain, it's a fascinating time for Columbus Crew fans.

It was a good 2018 season for Columbus, and without a doubt, it's a team in the mix for the 2019 campaign. One question the team has to address is whether multiple players can step up and match the goals Zardes tallied in 2018. That would certainly help the cause of getting to the MLS Cup final. With Trapp, Zardes, and Clark, along with Steffen in goal, it's a team with a lot of experience, and one that should be making a strong push throughout the season.

Overall Team Rating: 8.4

D.C. UNITED

Twitter: @dcunited
First season: 1996
MLS Cup: 4
US Open Cup: 3
Supporters' Shield: 4

Known For
Winning the MLS Cup four times
One of the original 10 MLS teams
Very loud fans
Bruce Arena
John Harkes
Eddie Pope
Jeff Agoos
Jaime Moreno
Ben Olsen
Chris Pontius
Wayne Rooney

A BRIEF TEAM HISTORY

While D.C. United is one of the original 10 teams from 1996, it's also one of the most successful, with four MLS Cups to date

(1996, 1997, 1999, and 2004). This is an organization rich with success from the early days of MLS, and it still has a lot of room to grow. Will it take 54 attempts to regain the MLS Cup? Surely the ownership circle would like it to occur a lot quicker. As one of the league's most storied franchises, one would think D.C. United will soon return to the top.

D.C. United is currently owned by Erick Thohir, who is originally from Indonesia, and Jason Levien, an American with experience in the past as CEO of the Memphis Grizzlies. In the team's early years, United was led by Bruce Arena, and he made MLS history as the first head coach to win the title in D.C.'s opening season.

In 1998, D.C. United won the CONCACAF Champions' Cup, a significant achievement. United has also captured the Supporters' Shield on four occasions (1997, 1999, 2006, and 2007).

US OPEN CUP

D.C. United, one of the best teams in MLS history, has won the US Open Cup three times (1996, 2008, and 2013).

FACTS ABOUT THEIR CITY

Washington DC—the home of the White House, the land of politics—has a population of around 6.1 million people in the greater metro area.

Beer is abundant around DC, and a few local beer makers are 3 Stars Brewing Company, DC Brau, and Atlas Brew Works. While fans enjoy these drinks, they can also stop by a few different restaurants around game time, which include The Dabney, Estadio, Blue Duck Tavern, and many others.

The D.C. United supporters' groups are known as Barra Brava, District Ultras, and Screaming Eagles.

WHERE THE TEAM IS TODAY: TACTICS AND STRATEGIES

In 2018, D.C. United was led offensively by the brilliant Wayne Rooney and the crafty Luciano Acosta, with the versatile Paul Arriola adding runs down the wing. As the 2019 season progresses, it's a team that will rely on quick combination passing. The acquisition of Rooney helped a great deal in this respect; his wealth of experience allowed him to guide the possession side of things with great ease, moving passes along with an eye for the moment (i.e., he knows exactly where the right pass should go at any given moment). Sometimes one player is a tactic and strategy all in one, and that's Rooney. He's like a coach on the field, a great presence orchestrating the guys on the field.

Defensively, in 2018, with the goalkeeping services of David Ousted and Bill Hamid, United used the 4-2-3-1 formation. For the most part, it was a team fighting to get out of the lower end of the pack, juggling success and failure around each corner. Things just weren't consistent enough.

All in all, 2018 was a good-ish season. On paper, it was not a good season, but the team wasn't that bad. With that said, United made a late run and ended up placing fourth in the Eastern Conference, thus qualifying for the playoffs during which it lost in the first round to Columbus.

With or without Rooney, United needs to improve matters on both sides of the ball. Without a doubt, 2019 represents a strong opportunity to fine tune a few things to find harmony between offense and defense and to be more consistent.

BEN OLSEN: A BRIEF COACHING PORTRAIT

Ben Olsen—the Virginia University standout—spent the majority of his professional career with D.C. United, and upon his retirement he immediately transitioned to the position of head coach. The last time D.C. United won the MLS Cup was in 2004. During the 2018 season, United—a team that had good talent in the form of Paul Arriola, Luciano Acosta and Wayne Rooney, and that played the game well—spent much of its time at the bottom of the Eastern Conference. It wasn't a horrible team, things just didn't go exactly as planned. (Despite a coach's best intentions, this happens from time to time.) And then, with a late run, United placed fourth in the Eastern Conference. Prior to this, consistency was an issue. This is something that Olsen and those around the franchise want to improve upon.

Don't be surprised to see a 4-2-3-1 formation; Olsen is a coach that stresses the importance of keeping good shape in the attack. Moving forward, with good talent available, 2019 is a great opportunity for Olsen and United to own the Eastern Conference.

KEY PLAYERS AND THEIR CHARACTERISTICS

Paul Arriola, Wayne Rooney, and Luciano Acosta

Paul Arriola—who has experience with USMNT—is a young attacking player that has good acceleration, crafty dribbling ability, an eye for passing, and a good overall feel for how the game should be played. Despite only being with D.C. United for a short time, the team should have him around for years to come, with an eye for getting the organization back into the MLS Cup championship game.

Wayne Rooney—one of England's best players in history, and one of the world's best attacking players—joined D.C. United recently after time with Everton and Manchester United. Andrew Das from *The New York Times* wrote that "Rooney's signing would harken back to the early days of MLS, when the league often signed players well past their prime for their name value as much as their soccer talent."[23] Still in his early thirties, Rooney has a lot to offer with a level of goal-scoring instincts that very few players have. He's also a great asset in terms of bringing fans in, along with trade value.

Rooney has stayed loyal to two clubs in the past, which is what D.C. United is counting on, but there's always the opportunity for a player like him to find a new deal out there. If he stays with United, good things should be around the corner.

Luciano Acosta is a crafty attacking midfielder from Argentina that D.C. United is hoping to keep around for years to come. He has many years left to play at a high level, and there's a chance he might be traded down the road, but for now, D.C. United can count on his smart passes around the box to guide the club in a positive direction.

KEY PLAYER STATS

(Total career goals with this club)

	Games Played	Goals	Scoring Percentage
Paul Arriola	39	8	20%
Wayne Rooney	21	12	57%
Luciano Acosta	95	18	18%

WHAT TO WATCH FOR ON TV: HOW BRADLEY, IBRAHIMOVIC, NAGBE, AND OTHERS PLAY

Here's the good thing about United being less than great last year. As most soccer fans know, United was once the top team in the east; this fact reminds us that MLS now has a wealth of history beginning to pile up. That's something to reflect upon! We can juxtapose United's season last year to its overall track record as a club which means that MLS is still alive and ticking, something that some people doubted back in the 1990s.

Let's go back twenty years to a time when United was the gold standard of the league. Back then, in the late 1990s, when soccer was still a sideshow on the great American sports landscape, the league was so new that it was sifting its way through unknown territory, creating new chapters and memories along the way. Essentially, it's great that MLS is now something with a past, something to reflect on, something that is continuing forward, and leading the way in the ongoing story that is American soccer (America's last athletic frontier). So that's the good news.

The bad news happens to be United's 2018 season, which, for the most part, wasn't very good (at least on paper); if you saw them play, things weren't completely dysfunctional; it was a team that played the game well. And, in fact, it eventually got fourth place in the Eastern Conference and made the MLS Playoffs. However, leading up to the somewhat surprising finish, United was struggling in the standings.

Regardless, as for the 2019 season, United is in a special place, one that is affording it an opportunity to recapture its glory days, to relive the great era of the late 1990s when United ruled the American soccer universe.

If Wayne Rooney sticks around, United has a great centerpiece to build around—a passer, a scorer, someone who can tackle as well. Take, for example, a game on August 12, 2018. D.C. United was tied 2-2 with Orlando City. In the dying moments of the second half, Rooney made a recovery run and tracked down an Orlando City player somewhere around midfield, tackled the ball from him, then looked downfield and delivered a long ball to the opposite side of the field where Acosta headed it in for the winner. It was a spectacular end to the game, a gift Rooney has waiting in his back pocket from time to time.

With players such as Rooney, Arriola, Yamil Asad, Ian Harkes, and Acosta potentially returning, and with new players brought in to steer things in a different direction, watch for D.C. United to launch a comeback, potentially of epic proportions.

Overall Team Rating: 8

This rating is based on United not doing well in the standings last season. However, it was playing the game well, which should push the rating to around 8.5. Making the 2018 MLS Playoffs is a plus as well. However, the majority of the season was more like a 7.7 or 7.8, hence 8 as the overall rating.

MONTREAL IMPACT

Twitter: @impactmontreal
First season: 2012
MLS Cup: 0
US Open Cup: 0
Supporters' Shield: 0

Known For
Dedicated fans
MLS Canadian expansion team
Winners of the Canadian Championship in 2013 and 2014
Andres Romero
Didier Drogba
Ignacio Piatti

A BRIEF TEAM HISTORY

Montreal Impact played its first MLS season in 2012. The Impact currently plays its games in Saputo Stadium, which holds around 20,000 people and, despite not having an MLS Cup in its trophy case yet, it's a team on the rise. Will it take Montreal 72 years to bring home the MLS Cup? Fans would likely want it to occur much sooner, while the club is setting a course to guide its ship in the right direction.

US OPEN CUP

To date, the Impact has not won a US Open Cup.

FACTS ABOUT THEIR CITY

Montreal has a population of around 1.7 million people in the city, a place known for speaking French above English.

Brasseur de Montreal might be a place locals enjoy beer for the games. Further options for fans are Restaurant Bonaparte, Restaurant Europea, and Verses Bistro, along with plenty of others. Keep an eye out for the supporters' groups that go by Ultras Montreal, 127 Montreal, and 1642 MTL.

WHERE THE TEAM IS TODAY: TACTICS AND STRATEGIES

Offensively, the 4-3-3 allows players to spread out evenly around the field, covering most areas. In 2018, it enabled Alejandro Silva, Samuel Piette, Ken Krolicki, and others to find connections, and it brought about decent results as the Impact were in the thick of things toward the end of the season.

Defensively, the 4-3-3 plays to the advantage of the team applying it. Defenders can pressure the ball at any position. In particular, the forwards can apply pressure to the defenders of an opposing team with more unity. This allows breathing room for defenders like Daniel Lovitz, Rudy Camacho, Rod Fanni, and

Bacary Sagna. With extra pressure applied to an opposing team's backline, the Impact defenders are able to sit back, analyze, and anticipate interceptions with more ease.

REMI GARDE: A BRIEF COACHING PORTRAIT

Remi Garde—who was born in France and who played with the French national team for a short time in the early 1990s—has found a place in Montreal, coaching a team hungry for a title. Prior to landing in Montreal, Remi coached Lyon and Aston Villa. Don't be surprised to see a 4-3-3 formation as Remi and company take on the Eastern Conference in 2019.

KEY PLAYERS AND THEIR CHARACTERISTICS

Ignacio Piatti and Samuel Piette

Ignacio Piatti is an offensive talent from Argentina whose skill is elegant with a touch of intuitive genius. His goal-scoring ability resembles a true South American artist at work.

Samuel Piette—born in Canada in 1994—is a midfielder with some experience playing in Spain, most recently with Club Deportivo Izarra. He's also got a number of games under his belt with the Canadian national team. With the Impact, Piette is one to watch in the middle of the field, distributing the ball throughout the 4-3-3 formation. Watch for Piette to step up and improve upon last year's progress.

KEY PLAYER STATS

(Total career goals with this club)

	Games Played	Goals	Scoring Percentage
Ignacio Piatti	124	63	50%
Samuel Piette	45	0	0%

WHAT TO WATCH FOR ON TV: HOW BRADLEY, IBRAHIMOVIC, NAGBE, AND OTHERS PLAY

Some of the players featured in 2018 included Matteo Mancosu, Alejandro Silva, Samuel Piette, Ken Krolicki, Daniel Lovitz, Rudy Camacho, Rod Fanni, Victor Cabrera, Bacary Sagna, Jukka Raitala, and Evan Bush in goal. It wasn't the best of years, but it definitely wasn't the worst, either.

With Ignacio Piatti around the goal, it would seem like good things should happen. Watch for Piatti working magic, along with support from the wings as the Impact looks to improve upon last season, and, with a strong effort to get out of the middle of the pack, it has a good chance to step closer to the MLS Cup title.

Overall Team Rating: 7.9

NEW ENGLAND REVOLUTION

Twitter: @NERevolution
First season: 1996
MLS Cup: 0
US Open Cup: 1
Supporters' Shield: 0

Known For
One of the original 10 MLS teams
Super loud fans
Super passionate fans
Steve Nicol
Brad Friedel
Alexi Lalas
Taylor Twellman
Chris Tierney

A BRIEF TEAM HISTORY

Amazingly, with all its success, Revolution has not won the MLS Cup yet, but it does have five second-place finishes. That's worth repeating: five second-place finishes—that's a lot. This is a team determined to get back to the final game and get its first title.

Revolution has been in the league since the beginning, and during its history there have been many good years, with an assortment of interesting coaches. The list includes Frank Stapleton, Thomas Rongen, Walter Zenga, Steve Nicol, Fernando Clavijo, Steve Nicol (again), Jay Heaps, Tom Soehn, and, last but not least, Brad Friedel.

US OPEN CUP

New England Revolution has one US Open Cup from 2007 after defeating FC Dallas to win the title.

FACTS ABOUT THEIR CITY

Boston has a population of around 4.6 million people in the greater metro area.

Samuel Adams, Trillium Brewing Company, Turtle Swamp Brewing, and Dorchester Brewing Company are a few local beers sure to be available around game time. Restaurants around the stadium that you might come across are Neptune Oyster, Davio's Northern Italian Steakhouse, Lincoln Tavern and Restaurant (South Boston, MA), and Row 34.

Circulating around home games, making their presence known, are the passionate supporters' groups known as The Midnight Riders, La Barra Revolution Latina, The Rebellion, and Rev Army.

WHERE THE TEAM IS TODAY: TACTICS AND STRATEGIES

Offensively, watch for Diego Fagundez in the attack, while elsewhere there should be support from Cristian Penilla and Teal Bunbury. While Bunbury likes balls played over the top, the team, at times, will participate in long balls out wide, changing the point of attack, with no real plan after that. It's a problem every team in the world has to deal with. A great ball is played out wide… now what? Furthermore, there's no real consistent attempt at a two-man game in possession. With that said, generally speaking, an attack has the tendency to fall dead with no combination passing sequences after a successful long ball is played out wide. If Revolution adjust this issue, better results should arrive, and balls played over the top to Bunbury will likely have more venom. Without a more constructive approach in possession, *you're just lobbing balls over the top to Bunbury*, which is like playing with a hope and a prayer (which will most likely end in disappointment).

Defensively, Chris Tierney and Claude Dielna were called upon in 2018 to keep things steady on the back line. Both players brought valuable experience, and replacing them will be a heavy task for Revolution moving forward.

BRAD FRIEDEL: A BRIEF COACHING PORTRAIT

Brad Friedel—who nonchalantly adopted a British accent from his time abroad—is a coach that might have a harder time overcoming his image as one of America's best all-time goalies—and that of the EPL—before people accept him as a coach of tantamount quality. There is also the added pressure he faces of literally telling people how to play on the field as an ex-goalie. An argument can be successfully made that goalies—like anybody—can understand the game; however, deep down, many people question the idea of an ex-keeper telling field players how to build chemistry together when they as goalies only watched it unfold, and never actually did such a thing.

Friedel stresses accountability with the team, as he has sought to bring in a new atmosphere and culture to the grounds. In doing so, don't be surprised to see a 4-2-3-1 formation as Friedel—an interesting guy—takes on the task of bringing New England back into the conversation as one of the elite teams in the league.

KEY PLAYERS AND THEIR CHARACTERISTICS

Scott Caldwell and Teal Bunbury

Do not accuse Scott Caldwell of a being a scoring threat, because he only seems to score every leap year. Caldwell, a local from Massachusetts, lends a hand in the midfield, and, since 2013, he has over 150 games for the Revolution, with some youth national team experience in his past as well as time spent with the University of Akron (Ohio), a very good soccer program.

Teal Bunbury is a veteran attacking player with both Canadian and American national team experience. Prior to joining New

England, he played with Sporting Kansas City, Rochester Thunder, and the Akron Zips.

KEY PLAYER STATS

(Total career goals with this club)

	Games Played	Goals	Scoring Percentage
Scott Caldwell	178	5	2%
Teal Bunbury	148	28	18%

WHAT TO WATCH FOR ON TV: HOW BRADLEY, IBRAHIMOVIC, NAGBE, AND OTHERS PLAY

New England Revolution can at times rattle opponents, then fall back on its heels, regressing to the middle of the pack quicker than you can drop a boatload of tea in the harbor.

The 2018 season saw a solid line-up, which included Brian Wright, Diego Fagundez, Cristian Penilla, Kelyn Rowe, Cristhian Machado, Scott Caldwell, Wilfried Zahibo, Brandon Bye, Jalil Anibaba, Michael Mancienne, Andrew Farrell, and Matt Turner in goal (with Brad Knighton as an option).

The 2019 season presents a strong challenge for New England, as it will try to find the right tone on the field. It's always hard to keep a team together, but, with a pretty good year in 2018, the Revolution will attempt to maintain the flow it built. Having said that, it may be hard to establish a firm position in the top three of the Eastern Conference, considering both New York squads are coming off of good years, and Atlanta might be even stronger during 2019.

Always a team to reckon with, the Revolution are special to watch; as an original MLS team from 1996, it has the inconvenient task of trying to find a way to snatch the MLS Cup for the first time. Such a task provides nothing but good old-fashioned drama.

Overall Team Rating: 8.0

NEW YORK CITY FC

Twitter: @NYCFC
First season: 2015
MLS Cup: 0
US Open Cup: 0
Supporters' Shield: 0

Known For
Insanely loud fans
Insanely passionate fans
Insanely dedicated fans
Andrea Pirlo
Maximiliano Moralez
David Villa

A BRIEF TEAM HISTORY

Though New York City FC does not have a trophy from the US Open Cup or MLS Cup, it does have a second-place finish for the Supporters' Shield in 2017. Not bad for a team with limited experience in the league. The team's first director was Claudio Reyna, who was a midfielder for Manchester City and the USMNT in past years. Without question, New York City FC wants to build toward the success that Manchester City has gained over the years. For a team with such a short history in the league, New York is on the fast track to success, with big signings— including World Cup champions Andrea Pirlo and David Villa— and big expectations await.

US OPEN CUP

To date, New York City FC has not won the US Open Cup.

FACTS ABOUT THEIR CITY

New York City has a population of around 8.5 million people in the city, with around 20 million people in the metropolitan area.

There are many sports teams in New York, including the Yankees, Mets, Knicks, Rangers, Islanders, Giants, Jets, and two MLS teams. New York has been the home to many interesting people, including Nikola Tesla, Spike Lee, Woody Allen, Pelé, and Beckenbauer, while New York City FC has provided a home to many talented players such as Pirlo and David Villa, who brought an artistic touch to the field.

Of the many places to grab a beer in New York City, fans might stumble across Rockaway Brewing Company, located in Long Island City, part of Queens. Making noise for NYCFC are the supporters' groups known as Chicken Bucket FC, The Third Rail, The Blue Ladies, Hearts of Oak, NYC12, and Bronx Football Social Club.

WHERE THE TEAM IS TODAY: TACTICS AND STRATEGIES

Offensively, NYCFC has a potent and smart attack guided by Maximiliano Moralez's passing ability, which can be very calm and effective. He lulls opponents to sleep with thoughtful play and then, in the blink of an eye, things tumble downfield toward the foot of David Villa, always waiting around goal where he only needs half a yard to place a low shot into the back of the net.

Defensively, with Maxime Chanot, Anton Tinnerholm, and Alexander Callens at the ready, New York City FC has a formidable unit that relieves pressure and distributes the ball in a timely fashion to Moralez and others for transitions. Other defenders featured in 2018 were Ben Sweat, Ronald Matarrita, Sebastien Ibeagha, and Sean Johnson presiding in goal (with Brad Stuver as an option). While New York City FC had a good season last year, expect to see much of the same on the defensive end as it makes a push to dominate the Eastern Conference. With the 4-3-3 formation—which NYCFC will likely use again—defensive pressure is evenly applied throughout the field, thus helping the defense as a whole.

DOMENEC TORRENT: A BRIEF COACHING PORTRAIT

Domenec Torrent is a Spanish-born coach with the task of taking New York City FC to higher levels, and hopefully, from the point of view of their fans, to the MLS Cup final. New to the job with New York FC, Torrent will likely guide his troops onto the field with a 4-3-3 formation, the favored approach of Pep Guardiola in past years. Torrent spent time around Pep and credits him and his approach as part of his own; positional play is important to Torrent, and the 4-3-3 is a great system to apply defensive pressure evenly throughout the field. (Watch out New York Red Bulls!) Under his direction, the team is pass oriented, looking to use possession throughout various channels to attain field dominance, with the goal of getting the ball into advantageous positions for Villa and supporting attackers.

KEY PLAYERS AND THEIR CHARACTERISTICS

David Villa, Maximiliano Moralez, and Thomas McNamara

David Villa—a former MLS MVP and World Cup champion with Spain—may have a few years left to offer NYCFC, if he can avoid injury. Should he remain active, he's a crafty, smart, and skillful scorer, using guile more than brute force to get the ball in the net.

Maximiliano Moralez, a midfielder from Argentina, has great first touch, with immaculate skill and technique delivered from a calm demeanor.

Thomas McNamara, the man with the long hair, always has a willingness to find an open teammate—and he'll throw a few goals in every once in a while, too.

KEY PLAYER STATS

(Total career goals with this club)

	Games Played	Goals	Scoring Percentage
David Villa	124	80	64%
Maximiliano Moralez	61	13	21%
Thomas McNamara	86	13	15%

WHAT TO WATCH FOR ON TV: HOW BRADLEY, IBRAHIMOVIC, NAGBE, AND OTHERS PLAY

Under Torrent, New York City FC is a team intent on using a possession-oriented approach to overwhelm opponents with passing combinations and quality of play to win, which was the case in 2018. A few players featured in 2018 included Ismael Tajouri-Shradi, Valentin Castellanos, Rodney Wallace, Jo Inge Berget, Tommy McNamara, David Villa, Jesus Medina, Ebenezer Ofori, Alexander Ring, and Maximiliano Moralez. If this team can stay together, watch for an explosive season in 2019 as NYCFC builds off of a brilliant year in 2018.

Overall Team Rating: 9.1

NEW YORK RED BULLS

Twitter: @NewYorkRedBulls
First season: 1996
MLS Cup: 0
US Open Cup: 0
Supporters' Shield: 3

Known For
One of the original 10 MLS teams
Formerly known as New York/New Jersey MetroStars
Insanely loud fans
Very passionate fans
Tab Ramos
Roberto Donadoni
Lothar Matthaus
Tim Howard
Clint Mathis
Juan Pablo Angel
Thierry Henry
Luis Robles
Bradley Wright-Phillips

A BRIEF TEAM HISTORY

In 1996, the New York/New Jersey MetroStars took the field, and in 2006, the name was changed to the New York Red Bulls. Despite a second-place finish in 2008, the team has not yet won the MLS Cup, and the goal remains the same—to reach the mountaintop, holding the trophy high, just as its rival D.C. United has done on previous occasions.

New York has never been short of exciting players. Plenty of top-level talent has passed through the halls of New York, including Tab Ramos, Roberto Donadoni, Lothar Matthaus, Tim Howard, Clint Mathis, and Thierry Henry.

Over the years, the Red Bulls have had interesting coaches, including Eddie Firmani, Carlos Queiroz, Carlos Alberto Parreira, Alfonso Mondelo, Bora Milutinovic, Octavio Zambrano, Bob Bradley, Mo Johnston, Richie Williams, Bruce Arena, Juan Carlos Osorio, Richie Williams (again), Hans Backe, Mike Petke, Jesse Marsch, and Chris Armas.

As coaches have come and gone, the Red Bulls have remained a quality team within the Eastern Conference. The 2018 season was dynamite for the Red Bulls, and they are looking to recapture that success in 2019 with stellar performances from Bradley Wright-Phillips up top and the midfield play of Tyler Adams and Kaku, backed up by a stern defense featuring Tim Parker and Kemar Lawrence.

US OPEN CUP

To date, the Red Bulls have not won the US Open Cup.

FACTS ABOUT THEIR CITY

New York City has a population of around 8.5 million people in the city, with around 20 million people in the metropolitan area.

Threes Brewing, out of Brooklyn, serves locally produced beer, which fans might enjoy before or after a game. Places to eat near where the Red Bulls play home games include Burger Bound, Spanish Tavern, Banzai Sushi, and Sakura Japan, among others.

The Red Bulls supporters' groups are Empire Supporters Club, Garden State Ultras, and Viking Army.

WHERE THE TEAM IS TODAY: TACTICS AND STRATEGIES

Offensively, the Red Bulls unite around Bradley Wright-Phillips to get the attack moving forward, often resulting in strong scoring chances. These chances were accentuated in 2018 with good passes coming from multiple players, including Tyler Adams and Alejandro Romero Gamarra (AKA Kaku).

Defensively, the Red Bulls will likely field a 4-2-3-1 formation, with a strong presence on the outside in Kemar Lawrence and solidified in the middle by Tim Parker.

The Red Bulls had a strong showing in 2018, one that emphasized heavy pressure on defense, which enabled the attack; this was, in a way, a synthesis for how they developed the offensive approach.

On the march to getting into the MLS Cup final, the Red Bulls will push the ball down the flanks, looking for good service into the box, with timely delivery, hoping to catch its opponent off guard. It has attained many goals with this approach to date, and from the looks of it, if the Red Bulls manage to stay on track, good things should happen. At times, with a lead, they can lose a little of their momentum, but with a sound roster, they hope to stay in flight, ahead of the pack in the Eastern Conference.

CHRIS ARMAS: A BRIEF COACHING PORTRAIT

Chris Armas replaced Jesse Marsch in 2018 (during the World Cup in Russia), and don't be surprised to see a 4-2-3-1 formation with a strong emphasis on defense as the Red Bulls surge forward.

Before Jesse Marsch left, he brought a lot to the table. Marsch—a Wisconsin native, who was born in 1973 and who was a standout player during his days at Princeton University—was a midfielder that played with D.C. United, Chicago Fire, and Chivas USA. A lot of the success he brought to the Red Bulls has been inherited by Armas.

Armas—a Bronx native who assisted Marsch with the Red Bulls—brings experience from his playing days with Chicago Fire and the USMNT. Under his guidance, the Red Bulls look to maintain their defensive prowess, which includes possibly the best outside back in MLS, Kemar Lawrence, who provides timely tackles. It's a team that wants to continue to increase scoring chances around goal by getting numbers up and using quick counterattacks, in order to remain a top team in the Eastern Conference.

KEY PLAYERS AND THEIR CHARACTERISTICS

Bradley Wright-Phillips, Kemar Lawrence, Tyler Adams, Kaku, and Tim Parker

The always-dangerous forward, Bradley Wright-Phillips—who was born in England and who brings with him plenty of professional experience from across the pond—has an ability to score goals, which is exactly what he's brought to the Red Bulls, scoring a ton of them. He's in second place for the all-time single-season scoring record, with 27. He's in that position with two other players, Roy Lassiter and Chris Wondolowski. (Josef Martinez surpassed 27 goals in 2018.) Wright-Phillips is quick and has a good sense of where to be in the box, where he plays with sound technique.

Adding some defense to the line-up is Kemar Lawrence, a very experienced player with the Jamaican national team. He brings a talented left foot to the table in the form of crosses and the occasional goal and relieves defensive pressure for the team which is crucial for counters.

Tyler Adams—a midfielder that has spent his career with the Red Bulls—played in the 2018 MLS All-Star Game. So far, he's had some experience with the USMNT. Born in 1999, he's a younger player; keep an eye out for him as the season progresses and beyond, as he might turn into a regular for the USMNT.

Alejandro Romero Gamarra (AKA Kaku) is a super-talented player, distributing the ball and getting everyone involved. Should he stay on board, the Red Bulls have a good creator with his touch on the ball.

Tim Parker—a well-built guy—is a central defender that keeps things steady, and he has already gained a brief amount of games with the USMNT. He also brings a lot of experience from the Vancouver Whitecaps.

KEY PLAYER STATS

(Total career goals with this club)

	Games Played	Goals	Scoring Percentage
Bradley Wright-Phillips	171	106	61%
Kemar Lawrence	96	4	4%
Tyler Adams	52	2	3%
Kaku	30	6	20%
Tim Parker	29	1	3%

WHAT TO WATCH FOR ON TV: HOW BRADLEY, IBRAHIMOVIC, NAGBE, AND OTHERS PLAY

The Red Bulls are a big-name team, with past players such as Thierry Henry, the experienced World Cup champion from France. They've created a strong rivalry with their crosstown neighbors, New York City FC, and there are other threats in the East—such as New England Revolution, D.C. United, and Philadelphia Union—constantly knocking at the door.

The Red Bulls are a team on the move, with attacking power and the strength in defense to carry leads to the last whistle. On its quest for the MLS Cup, the Red Bulls use the wings and counterattack with energy. There is security at outside defense with Kemar Lawrence, and he should continue to do good things in that position, inspiring others with tackles. Getting the ball in attacking positions for Bradley Wright-Phillips is the main course of action, and, with his adept scoring touch, good things usually happen around goal.

Overall Team Rating: 8.9

ORLANDO CITY SC

Twitter: @OrlandoCitySC
First season: 2015
MLS Cup: 0
US Open Cup: 0
Supporters' Shield: 0

Known For
Being an expansion team
Revitalizing soccer in Florida
Kaka
Brek Shea
Dom Dwyer
Kingston (the mascot)

A BRIEF TEAM HISTORY

The first goal scored for Orlando City SC in Major League Soccer was by Kaka, in 2015. Since then, Orlando City SC has not won the MLS Cup, nor has it won the US Open Cup or even the Supporters' Shield, but these milestones are on its list of things to do. You can bet on that. Orlando City SC's first MLS game in 2015 marks a comeback for soccer in Florida. Previously, Tampa

Bay and Miami each tried their hand at MLS, and eventually folded. Orlando has led the way back into the league, and, someday soon, expect to see Orlando's in-state neighbor, Miami, rise again, with the help of David Beckham. As for Orlando, they'll be looking forward to that rivalry, which will certainly help liven up the soccer scene in the great state of Florida.

Waiting for Miami, and any other team that comes to town, is the team mascot, Kingston, a muscular lion who stands on two feet; wears a purple team shirt, black adidas track pants, and purple shoes; and sports dreadlocks.

US OPEN CUP

To date, Orlando City SC has not won the US Open Cup.

FACTS ABOUT THEIR CITY

Orlando has a population of around 2.3 million people in the greater metro area. It's known as a great vacation destination, with Disney World as the prime attraction.

In Orlando, there are a few soccer academies, including My Soccer Academy, Orange Soccer Academy, and R9 Ronaldo Academy.

When it comes to beer, Orlando isn't necessarily thought of as a great beer-making kingdom, but if you're going to an Orlando City SC game and feel like having a local beer, Orlando Brewing might be a place to drop by before or after a game.

Supporters' groups loyal to Orlando City—and sure to be seen around home games—include Iron Lion Firm and The Ruckus.

WHERE THE TEAM IS TODAY: TACTICS AND STRATEGIES

The 2018 season wasn't the best for Orlando, to say the least. Offensively, during 2018, a few players trickled in and out, including Cristian Higuita, Oriol Rosell, Carlos Ascues, Chris Mueller, David Josue Colman Escobar, Will Johnson, Tony Rocha, Yoshimar Yotun, Sacha Kljestan, Dom Dwyer, and Mohamed El Monir. Orlando City SC has been seen playing a 4-3-3 and 4-2-3-1; based on 2018's results, this needs to be revisited. Defensively, the 2018 season featured Jonathan Spector, Scott Sutter, Shane O'Neill, Amro Tarek, PC, and Joe Bendik in goal (with Earl Edwards Jr. as an option). Expect to see some drastic changes throughout the 2019 MLS season.

Kljestan was brought in to help but was unable to transform the season into a winning record. Can blame be put on Kljestan or Spector (who was also brought in to help)? It's hard to say. They both have limited experience with the team. (Sometimes as many as three years are needed to get things rolling.) It's also a franchise that hasn't won the MLS Cup yet. It's a team without any major achievements, and any one player can't necessarily fix the problem.

The larger issue that looms overhead is that of Orlando's future as a team. Is it a franchise soon to fold? Based on the results of 2018 and the lack of chemistry on the field, it seems like a difficult task to keep fans interested for long. Time will tell. There's a lot Orlando executives need to think about.

JAMES O'CONNOR: A BRIEF COACHING PORTRAIT

Born in 1979, James O'Connor is a 5'8" lad from Dublin, Ireland that played professionally as a midfielder for a handful of teams, including Sheffield Wednesday. Prior to taking on the Orlando City SC job, O'Connor had success coaching Louisville City FC.

Orlando City SC is O'Connor's first MLS head coaching position. Players say he's an intense coach, and he seems to agree with this assessment. That's always a good start—know what you bring to the table.

His transition to coaching Orlando City SC has been trying, to say the least. Hopefully, 2018 was a transition year, one that in many respects needs to be forgotten. Yet, all the same, O'Connor can draw on the successes and failures of 2018 for a bit of wisdom as he moves forward with the 2019 campaign.

KEY PLAYERS AND THEIR CHARACTERISTICS

Dom Dwyer, Will Johnson, and Sacha Kljestan

In January 2018, Dom Dwyer arrived in Orlando as part of a three-year deal, with plans to add his goal-scoring touch to a squad on the verge of doing great things. According Alicia DelGallo at the *Orland Sentinel*, "details of the contract were not released, but Dwyer will be a designated player on Orlando City's roster. His average guaranteed salary for 2017 was $668,750, according to numbers released by the MLS Players Union. In July, the Lions traded a then-MLS record $1.6 million of allocation money—$400,000 in general allocation money and $500,000 in targeted allocation money, plus up to $700,000 in future allocation money based on incentives—to Sporting Kansas City for Dwyer, but he was in his final contract year and had not yet signed a new deal."[24] Dwyer—who will provide a lot of activity up front with a good left foot and the ability to score on headers—has some games under his belt with the USMNT, and Orlando is hoping to get good results from him in the years to come.

Will Johnson is a Canadian midfielder who had a long stint with Real Salt Lake in the past. Watch for Johnson distributing passes and organizing in the midfield with the intent of improving the record from last season.

The *Orlando Sentinel* captured the news of Sacha Kljestan's arrival to Orlando City SC, reporting that "in 2018, Dwyer will have US national team midfielder and MLS assist leader Sacha Kljestan feeding him the ball. Orlando City announced Kljestan's signing Tuesday, getting him from the New York Red Bulls in exchange for Colombian striker Carlos Rivas and homegrown defender Tommy Redding."[25]

KEY PLAYER STATS

(Total career goals with this club)

	Games Played	Goals	Scoring Percentage
Dom Dwyer	38	17	44%
Will Johnson	54	3	5%
Sacha Kljestan	30	6	20%

WHAT TO WATCH FOR ON TV: HOW BRADLEY, IBRAHIMOVIC, NAGBE, AND OTHERS PLAY

Orlando has a great opportunity to turn things around with a spectacular 2019 MLS season. However, whether this happens is yet to be seen. In 2018, some of the players featured included Cristian Higuita, Oriol Rosell, Carlos Ascues, Chris Mueller, David Josue Colman Escobar, Will Johnson, Tony Rocha, Yoshimar Yotun, Sacha Kljestan, Dom Dwyer, Mohamed El Monir, Jonathan Spector, Scott Sutter, Shane O'Neill, Amro Tarek, PC, and Joe Bendik.

Kljestan, Spector, and Dwyer—should they remain on board— are key fixtures that have the responsibility of steering this ship in the right direction. Optimists might say that things are looking up and that, if they stay on the front foot and make the extra pass, things should improve. Skeptics—who recognize that Orlando has no legacy to work with, struggles to recruit talent, and needs a miracle to turn things around—might offer something like, "Good luck with that."

Orlando's road record in 2018 was less than desirable. Improving this will be vitally important in order to step forward as a viable team for the playoffs. The situation Orlando is in now is dire; it's not a good place. Teams fold over bad seasons, disarray, and lack of results. Orlando fans should be riveted. Times like these make or break a team or a franchise. How much more exciting can it get? Drama. It's good for the game and good for the league.

Overall Team Rating: 6.8

PHILADELPHIA UNION

Twitter: @PhilaUnion
First season: 2010
MLS Cup: 0
US Open Cup: 0
Supporters' Shield: 0

Known For
Insanely loud fans
Sebastien Le Toux
Conor Casey
Jack McInerney
Chris Pontius
Zac MacMath
Fafa Picault
Alejandro Bedoya

A BRIEF TEAM HISTORY

Philadelphia Union, a team on the rise, came into existence in 2008, eventually playing its first MLS game in 2010. Throughout much of the 20th century, Philadelphia has been an active area for youth soccer—not to mention the fact that it's a major market city—and some people were surprised that it took them so long to establish a team in MLS. To date, the organization has not won the MLS Cup. Each year the Union has had its eye on that prize, and, with a good season in 2018, it's getting one step closer. The team is under the ownership of Keystone Sports and Entertainment LLC, and the games are played at Talen Energy Stadium, which has a capacity of around 18,500.

US OPEN CUP

At this point in time, Philadelphia Union has not won the US Open Cup.

FACTS ABOUT THEIR CITY

Philadelphia has a population of around 6 million people in the greater metro area. Yards Brewing Company, Saint Benjamin Brewing Company, Second District Brewing Company, and Evil Genius Beer Company provide beer which is available for fans around game time. Sons of Ben is a supporters' group that brings energy to home games.

WHERE THE TEAM IS TODAY: TACTICS AND STRATEGIES

Offensively, the Union is a team that maintains the ball in possession from the backline, looking to insert passes forward to further an attack towards goal. Simple, yes, but the Union did pretty well in 2018, keeping itself within the middle of the pack. It's a team that has players that can move down the line, and along with the defensive pressure it applies, which amps up around midfield, it has the potential to create quick counters. An out-and-out barrage of goals is currently not on the table for the Union—as it is with Atlanta—but the Union will apply steady pressure to establish a presence around its opponent's goal. Wow factor, no. Steadiness, yes.

I predict that the Union's 2019 season will reflect a lot of the previous year; it will remain a middle-of-the-pack team with good results, but nothing incredibly groundbreaking...at least not yet. Currently, steady seems to be preferred over ostentatious; considering the appetite Philadelphia fans have for their sports teams, a few trades might be in order to spruce things up. Philadelphia is a city that demands greatness, and, as things move forward in 2019, it wouldn't be surprising to see the franchise tinker with the lineup.

JIM CURTIN: A BRIEF COACHING PORTRAIT

Jim Curtin is a Pennsylvania native that spent a large time playing professionally as a defender with Chicago Fire. As leader of the Union, he is responsible for delivering the MLS Cup. To that end, don't be surprised to see a 4-2-3-1 or 4-3-3 formation. His team applies swift pressure defensively, while systematically inserting thoughtful possession—leaning towards possession with a purpose—throughout the attack and using the wings with speed when possible.

KEY PLAYERS AND THEIR CHARACTERISTICS

Fafa Picault, Alejandro Bedoya, and Andre Blake

Fafa Picault is an attacking player in his late twenties that has contributed on the goal front for the Union during the time he's been with the club. With him getting more goals, the team has a chance to be competitive in the Eastern Conference and to make a run for the playoffs.

Alejandro Bedoya is a player usually found on the outside as a midfielder. He's had a ton of experience with the USMNT, and he brings leadership to the group.

In 2016, Andre Blake—the talented keeper from Jamaica—won the MLS Goalkeeper of the Year Award. As ESPN said, "With an average of 24 percent of the vote, Blake, 25, beat out the New York Red Bulls' Luis Robles (14 percent) and the Colorado Rapids' Tim Howard (13 percent)."[26] As one of the top goalies in the league, Blake gives the Union a steady hand in goal as they make a push for the MLS Cup.

KEY PLAYER STATS

(Total career goals with this club)

	Games Played	Goals	Scoring Percentage
Fafa Picault	57	17	29%
Alejandro Bedoya	71	6	8%
Andre Blake	98	0	0%

WHAT TO WATCH FOR ON TV: HOW BRADLEY, IBRAHIMOVIC, NAGBE, AND OTHERS PLAY

On its quest to reach the championship game and hold the MLS Cup, the Union is a team on the rise. It's hungry for the title, and its fan base is eager to see it come to fruition. Watch for a steady attack that begins with defenders that possess the ball with purpose, wingers that can pose a speedy threat from time to time and a group approach to winning the ball back, which, if things work out in the team's favor, should result in a good counter. Although the Union are not a team that will dazzle you with South American skill, it's a group with talent, ready to compete with whoever is in front of them.

Overall Team Rating: 7.9

TORONTO FC

Twitter: @torontofc
First season: 2007
MLS Cup: 1
US Open Cup: 0
Supporters' Shield: 1

Known For
Winning the MLS Cup
Insanely passionate fans
Greg Vanney
Michael Bradley
Marky Delgado
Sebastian Giovinco

A BRIEF TEAM HISTORY

In 2016, Toronto took a second-place finish in the MLS Cup. Then, in 2017, Toronto FC won the MLS Cup for the first and only time to date. Two great years. However, the 2018 season was not one to write home about. Now, with a talented team that had a rough year, it's all about rebuilding, with an eye for getting back on top.

During Toronto's short time within the league—and as the first Canadian team to join MLS—it has risen to the top with the help of a passionate fan base. In fact, at BMO Field, where games are currently played, the loud Canadian fans quickly asserted their presence, making Toronto one of the toughest places to play on the road.

US OPEN CUP

To date, Toronto has not won the US Open Cup.

FACTS ABOUT THEIR CITY

Toronto has a population of around 5.9 million people in the greater metro area. Although hockey remains the most popular sport throughout Canada and the Toronto Maple Leafs are the pre-eminent team in town, soccer has entrenched itself within the inner fabric of Toronto society in a big way. While Toronto FC has found recent success (reaching the MLS Cup championship game in 2016 and winning it in 2017), CBC News reported that "enthusiasm appears to still be strong for the team, as CBC Toronto has learned that 99 percent of last year's season ticket holders have become season ticket holders this year as well."[27]

There's a lot of excitement in the air for the 2019 season as the Toronto fan base exudes passion. Supporters' groups for Toronto FC include Inebriatti, Red Patch Boys, and U-Sector.

If *Strange Brew*—featuring Rick Moranis and Dave Thomas—was an accurate indication of the love affair Canadians have with drinking, a number of local beer options are available for fans come game day, including, but not limited to, Steam Whistle Brewing, Left Field Brewery, and Junction Craft Brewing. Along with beer, restaurants are highly prevalent in the vast metropolitan area of Toronto, including Victor Restaurant, Arriba Restaurant, Penelope Restaurant, George Restaurant, and many others.

WHERE THE TEAM IS TODAY: TACTICS AND STRATEGIES

Toronto will likely field what looks to be a 4-3-1-2 formation, or possibly a 5-3-2 or even a 5-4-1.

Offensively, led by Sebastian Giovinco, Toronto has a patient, skillful, and methodic buildup with skillful interplay which allows them to break through the opponent's defense with interesting passes around the box. Jay Chapman, Jonathan Osorio, Liam Frazer, Jon Bakero, Jordan Hamilton, Jozy Altidore, Lucas Janson, Victor Vasquez, and Marky Delgado helped in this regard during 2018.

Defensively, Toronto applies good pressure, and it looks to keep the ball away from their opponent as a means of defense, which is good most of the time. Michael Bradley, a good defender, helps in this regard with his veteran experience. Some of the defenders from 2018 included Ryan Telfer, Justin Morrow, and Nick Hagglund. However, 2018 didn't turn out as planned. As a result, despite Toronto having two great years leading into 2018, don't be surprised to see big lineup changes.

If the team remains roughly the same, with minimal changes and injuries, and, more importantly, if Giovinco stays on board, then it'll be a team back in the front end of the standings.

GREG VANNEY: A BRIEF COACHING PORTRAIT

Greg Vanney, a former UCLA Bruin, played as a defender with an assortment of professional teams, including two stints with LA Galaxy, and had a significant amount of time with the USMNT as well.

Toronto plays smart, with a structured approach to passing. Even if things are down, it's a team with a plan and, with the leadership of Vanney, Toronto sees itself as a contender for the next few years.

KEY PLAYERS AND THEIR CHARACTERISTICS

Michael Bradley, Sebastian Giovinco, and Marky Delgado

Michael Bradley is a player that one might argue plays like a coach's son. That's because he is a coach's son—his father, Bob Bradley, currently coaches Los Angeles FC. Being raised around high-level soccer has made an impression on Michael, as he leads Toronto with a coach's eye, always looking to pass and distribute the ball effectively, and with a guiding hand that is based in tactical awareness.

Sebastian Giovinco is arguably one of the best players in MLS history. The Italian is blessed with craft and guile which enable him to step around defenders with smart and decisive movement, and he's always creating danger around the opponent's goal. In subtle ways, he's the type of player that makes the game interesting—which causes true soccer fans to get excited for his next performance.

Marky Delgado is a young player from California who potentially looks to be in line to get more reps with the USMNT. As a guiding force in Toronto's midfield, watch for him to distribute the ball and play off of Bradley as the 2019 season moves on.

KEY PLAYER STATS

(Total career goals with this club)

	Games Played	Goals	Scoring Percentage
Michael Bradley	136	8	5%
Sebastian Giovinco	114	68	59%
Marky Delgado	102	10	9%

WHAT TO WATCH FOR ON TV: HOW BRADLEY, IBRAHIMOVIC, NAGBE, AND OTHERS PLAY

Keep an eye on the rising talent of Ayo Akinola, a young American player from Detroit, Michigan. He has a promising future as an attacking player, and Toronto is looking to get a lot out of him down the road.

Toronto is a team that passes the ball well, guided in the midfield by Michael Bradley. With Sebastian Giovinco orchestrating things up front with a creative touch, they're a team to be reckoned with in the Eastern Conference. Toronto is looking to keep its MLS Cup championship run of 2017 going strong, though, with other teams making a valiant push in their conference, they might have to reevaluate a few things to remain a threat.

Overall Team Rating: 7.2

FC CINCINNATI

Twitter: @fccincinnati
First season: 2019
MLS Cup: 0
US Open Cup: 0
Supporters' Shield: 0

Known For
Being a brand new MLS team
Very passionate fans

A BRIEF TEAM HISTORY

Without any history in the MLS, FC Cincinnati is a brand new team, kicking off its inaugural season in America's top soccer league in the 2019 MLS season. Previously, FC Cincinnati had good years in the USL. The owner of the team, Carl Lindner III, is counting on his club to take advantage of its fresh start and an assortment of talent, including the likes of Forrest Lasso, Corben Bone, and Fanendo Adi.

US OPEN CUP

To date, FC Cincinnati does not have a US Open Cup.

FACTS ABOUT THEIR CITY

Cincinnati has a population of around 295,000 to 300,000 people. For years, fans have enjoyed the Bengals and Reds. FC Cincinnati, now a part of Major League Soccer, has joined the group of top-level teams, which is a remarkable bit of history for the city. For beers out of Cincinnati, try Streetside Brewery and 13 Below Brewery, among others. Beer is a well-appreciated drink in Ohio, and Cincinnati has great options for fans at game time.

WHERE THE TEAM IS TODAY: TACTICS AND STRATEGIES

Starting out fresh in its first MLS season, Cincinnati is a team with a lot to prove. With no previous experience in MLS, this section will remain unresolved for now. However, as the season progresses, it will be a group that finds its way through a forest of experienced clubs eager to get a win over a brand new team.

The best option for Cincinnati is to keep things simple, concentrate on fundamentals, establish a style, find a will to win, stay confident on defense, anticipate on defense (do not react on defense), fight for tackles, and stay together as a team. Mistakes will happen. Losses will likely build up.

In order to find wins, the mindset of the coaches and players should be one that establishes creativity on offense within an atmosphere that allows players to make mistakes. Players that are afraid to make mistakes get tense and don't perform well. Overcoming this potential obstacle might be Cincinnati's biggest challenge.

ANTHONY HUDSON: A BRIEF COACHING PORTRAIT

Stepping into the 2019 MLS season, Cincinnati will be led by coach Alan Koch, who is originally from South Africa.

KEY PLAYERS AND THEIR CHARACTERISTICS

Forrest Lasso, Corben Bone, and Fanendo Adi

Forrest Lasso, originally from North Carolina, is a defender with experience from FC Cincinnati in the USL.

Corben Bone, a midfielder who was born in Texas, has some experience with Chicago Fire and Philadelphia Union. He also spent time with FC Cincinnati in the USL.

Fanendo Adi is a forward from Nigeria that spent some time with Portland Timbers before joining FC Cincinnati in the USL.

KEY PLAYER STATS

(Total career goals with this club)

	Games Played	Goals	Scoring Percentage
Forrest Lasso	TBD	TBD	0%
Corben Bone	TBD	TBD	0%
Fanendo Adi	TBD	TBD	0%

WHAT TO WATCH FOR ON TV: HOW BRADLEY, IBRAHIMOVIC, NAGBE, AND OTHERS PLAY

FC Cincinnati is counting on a great rivalry with its neighbors in Columbus. However its opening MLS season turns out, this should be an epic year for Cincinnati, though questions will arise. Will the quality of play be good enough? Will ticket sales be consistent enough for the team to survive? Will the team be able to equal the accomplishments of Atlanta United and win the MLS Cup in its second season? The latter is a high bar for any team. What Atlanta has accomplished is unique. Minnesota, a new team as well, has not come close to Atlanta's success. For Cincinnati to jump in the league and head straight for the MLS Cup championship is asking a lot. For now, Cincinnati will be seeking good results. In the bigger picture, it's a franchise that is helping to advance the growth of MLS and soccer in general throughout America. In terms of winning seasons and chasing the elusive MLS Cup, the ongoing story of Cincinnati will be exciting to watch.

Overall Team Rating: To Be Determined

With no previous track record in MLS it's tricky to award an Overall Team Rating. For now, FC Cincinnati can have a Gentleman's 7.

COLORADO RAPIDS

Twitter: @ColoradoRapids
First season: 1996
MLS Cup: 1
US Open Cup: 0
Supporters' Shield: 0

Known For
Being one of the original 10 MLS teams
Very passionate fans
Marcelo Balboa
Chris Henderson
Mark Chung
Pablo Mastroeni
Conor Casey
Tim Howard

A BRIEF TEAM HISTORY

One of the original 10 MLS teams in 1996, the talented and determined Rapids won the MLS Cup back in 2010. Although the Rapids were an original franchise and despite being centrally located, the Rapids feel somewhat sequestered from the rest of the league. However, it is a franchise that has represented the league well and given its fans a great deal to cheer about.

Throughout the years, the head coaching list for the Rapids has included Bob Houghton, Roy Wegerle, Glenn Myernick, Tim Hankinson, Fernando Clavijo, Gary Smith, Oscar Pareja, Pablo Mastroeni, Steve Cooke, and Anthony Hudson.

US OPEN CUP

To date, the Rapids are seeking its first US Open Cup.

FACTS ABOUT THEIR CITY

The great state of Colorado is a place of government-constructed underground worlds, amazing beer, world-class ski resorts, and the legendary Denver Broncos. The greater metro area of Denver has a population of around 2.8 million people.

The Rapids operate out of Commerce City, just outside of Denver, and the games are played in Dick's Sporting Goods Park. A regular presence at home games is the Centennial 38 supporters' group. A few beers available for fans in and around the greater Denver area include Lost Highway Brewing Company, Epic Brewing Company, Lowdown Brewery, Our Mutual Friend Brewing, and Blue Moon Brewing Company.

WHERE THE TEAM IS TODAY: TACTICS AND STRATEGIES

It wasn't the best year for the one-time MLS Cup champs. Although the Rapids' past season was a shipwreck, the team is fighting to return to the top of the standings—and to the MLS Cup championship. What it has right now is hope, and a feeling of getting back to a place where it thinks it should be.

Offensively, watch for the Rapids to use a team effort, working the ball down the pitch with a mix of styles reflecting that of Germany and England. Although asking the team to score 108 goals in a season may indeed be asking a lot, it's a team that can achieve greatness, and, based on last season, simply getting to the top five of the Western Conference would be a big improvement. At that point, scoring a ton of goals might be within the realm of possibility.

Defensively, the Rapids are structured with an eye for counters, while it's a team that seizes opportunities to create deflections and loose balls whenever possible. From 2018, some defenders that were available included Kortne Ford of the United States, Deklan Wynne and Tommy Smith of New Zealand, and Danny Wilson of Scotland. The 2019 season might be a lot of the same, or it might be an opportunity to bring in new options.

ANTHONY HUDSON: A BRIEF COACHING PORTRAIT

Anthony Hudson was born in Seattle, Washington, and has had an interesting coaching history, having led Bahrain and New Zealand in the past. Can he lead the Rapids back to the top? That is yet to be seen.

Don't be surprised to see a 4-3-1-2 (which, depending how you look at it, is pretty much a 4-4-2) or possibly a 4-3-3 formation as Hudson looks to get his team back on track. The 4-3-3 seemed to be the lineup in use during Colorado's 6-0 loss to Real Salt Lake on August 25, 2018, so there might be some second-guessing when it comes to the 4-3-3. Time will tell.

KEY PLAYERS AND THEIR CHARACTERISTICS

Tim Howard, Giles Barnes, Jack Price, and Johan Blomberg

Tim Howard, the USMNT goalie for many years and who has World Cup experience to boot, brings a heavy dose of expertise to the lineup. He is fortunate to have played in the EPL for many years, with stops at Manchester United and Everton. He's thought to be one of the best goalies around, and, despite his age, he continues to be a solid choice in net.

Giles Barnes has recently joined the Rapids and brings experience from playing in England and with the Jamaican national team.

As an attacking player, he looks to add his scoring touch to the offense.

Jack Price is an English player that spent a lot of time with Wolverhampton Wanderers. He's relatively new to Colorado, but, should he stay on board, watch for him at center mid distributing the ball throughout the field, while keeping order on the defensive side of the ball.

Johan Blomberg is a midfielder from Sweden. Watch for Blomy distributing the ball to teammates in an all-out effort to turn this shipwreck around.

KEY PLAYER STATS

(Total career goals with this club)

	Games Played	Goals	Scoring Percentage
Tim Howard	75	0	0%
Giles Barnes	12	0	0%
Jack Price	31	1	3%
Johan Blomberg	24	0	0%

WHAT TO WATCH FOR ON TV: HOW BRADLEY, IBRAHIMOVIC, NAGBE, AND OTHERS PLAY

The defensive backline from 2018 certainly can't be blamed for everything last season. After all, who should receive blame for finishing second to last in the Western Conference? Sometimes it's best to hit the reset button. Should Kortne Ford, Deklan Wynne, Tommy Smith, and Danny Wilson remain with the team for 2019, they might have the advantage of hindsight, learning from 2018 and moving forward with confidence. This will be an interesting development to watch throughout the upcoming season.

In the midfield, the talented Kellyn Acosta arrived from Dallas during 2018. Keep an eye on how Colorado utilizes him throughout the year.

Will 2019 be Colorado's great comeback season? A return to the top? We'll wait and see. Colorado has a lot of promise, and its goal is to recapture the MLS Cup. Along the way, it's a team that attacks the wings, and concentrates a firm effort on defense, with guidance from Danny Wilson, Tommy Smith, and Jack Price. But, as was the case in 2018, things haven't exactly come out as planned. With some retooling, Colorado is looking to mount a comeback, as it looks to improve over the next few years.

Overall Team Rating: 7.2

FC DALLAS

Twitter: @FCDallas
First season: 1996
MLS Cup: 0
US Open Cup: 2
Supporters' Shield: 1

Known For
Being one of the original 10 MLS teams
Insanely loud fans
Very dedicated fans
Oscar Pareja
Eddie Johnson
Jason Kreis
Kenny Cooper
Michael Barrios

A BRIEF TEAM HISTORY

Dallas came into the league back in 1996, and it has had some very good years, earning the Supporters' Shield and US Open Cup along the way. With talented players from the past—including Jason Kreis, the versatile scorer; Kenny Cooper, the presence in the box; and Carlos Ruiz, the crafty and controversial Guatemalan goal scorer—it's a team constantly looking to stay relevant. In doing so, FC Dallas is looking to acquire more talent in the days to come on its quest for the MLS Cup, which has eluded it thus far. But, with a good product on the field, it'll get there sometime soon. In 2005, the team began playing its games at Toyota Stadium, located in Frisco, Texas.

As of 2018, the team owner was Clark Hunt (son of the great Lamar Hunt, who was so instrumental with soccer in the United States). Clark was born in Dallas and has been very active in Major League Soccer over the years. Under his guidance, Oscar Pareja coached during the 2018 MLS season—a phenomenal year for Dallas—and it's a team that intends on repeating it.

US OPEN CUP

Dallas has won the US Open Cup twice.

FACTS ABOUT THEIR CITY

Dallas has a population of around 7.2 million people in the greater metro area. With fans that love their sports and with a rich soccer tradition, Dallas is a place that's laid back, and people can enjoy the games with an assortment of local beers, with options from Community Beer Company, Four Corners Brewing Company, and Oak Highlands Brewery.

Come game time, a few FC Dallas supporters' groups that show up are the Dallas Beer Guardians, and El Matador. There are plenty of great restaurants for people to flock to around game time, and some of those are Rodeo Goat, The Grape Restaurant, Ocean Prime, and, of course, a few Texas-style BBQ joints, including Lockhart Smokehouse BBQ, Mike Anderson's Barbeque, Sammy's Bar-B-Q, and Peggy Sue BBQ.

WHERE THE TEAM IS TODAY: TACTICS AND STRATEGIES

Defensively, Dallas applies pressure quickly to alleviate the opponent's attack. Like any team, Dallas wants to limit errors in the box that might lead to shots for the opposing team. Matt Hedges is a solid figure in the back, one that can diffuse tricky situations with timely tackles.

Offensively, Dallas enjoyed a fantastic season last year. It's a group that strings passes together, attacks the wings, and applies pressure as a cohesive unit to create scoring chances. It's a team with many threats on the attack, including but not limited to Michael Barrios and Maximiliano Urruti.

Don't be surprised to see a 4-2-3-1 or potentially a 4-3-3 formation, with a steady, potent attack from all angles, a tactic that brought Dallas much success last season.

OSCAR PAREJA: A BRIEF COACHING PORTRAIT

Oscar Pareja is a former midfielder that played a handful of games with the Colombian national team, and he also played a few years with Dallas before leading from the sidelines.

Under his guidance, Dallas takes advantage of transitions, with multi-faceted contributions coming from a group rich in talent. Pareja led the team to great results in 2018. With that success, he has a firm platform to operate from moving forward.

KEY PLAYERS AND THEIR CHARACTERISTICS

Michael Barrios, Paxton Pomykal, and Reggie Cannon

Michael Barrios is the speedy winger from Colombia that gets down the line and into the box, often causing problems for opposing defenses.

Paxton Pomykal, born in 1999, is a young player to watch out for. He is a Texas native and product of the FC Dallas Academy. Despite not playing much yet, a source says he's a young talent that brings hope for the future to the table—someone Dallas is looking to keep around for a few years.

Reggie Cannon is a young defender that Dallas sees as a future asset for the team as the next few years roll around. He's part of this young crop of players that have been put in place to produce results in an ever-competitive league.

KEY PLAYER STATS

(Total career goals with this club)

	Games Played	Goals	Scoring Percentage
Michael Barrios	126	25	19%
Paxton Pomykal	8	0	0%
Reggie Cannon	34	1	2%

WHAT TO WATCH FOR ON TV: HOW BRADLEY, IBRAHIMOVIC, NAGBE, AND OTHERS PLAY

Director of Media Services Jason Minnick explained that FC Dallas prides itself on players that come up through the FC Dallas Academy; such a player is Paxton Pomykal and the hope is that he'll bring big results in the near future. (Kellyn Acosta was recently traded; he was another player that went through the FC Dallas Academy, and, who knows, maybe someday he'll get traded back to Dallas.)

Playing out of Toyota Stadium, this young team often relies on skill and determination to see wins through. It's a team that has a good amount of energy, and this, coupled with the right direction, is a good combination for success down the road. Maximiliano Urruti, Dominique Badji (unless he's merely an ephemeral acquisition from 2018), Matt Hedges, Reto Ziegler, Carlos Gruezo, and Victor Ulloa comprise some of the league's most potent all-around talent from 2018 that Dallas can throw at opponents this season. There is also potentially a good future with Pablo Aranguiz of Chile (should Dallas hold on to him), a player that could add more strength and depth to the midfield. Should this unit stay intact, a lot can be accomplished by Dallas in terms of keeping the league exciting with a sound structure of talent, and while chasing glory in the form of the MLS Cup.

Overall Team Rating: 9.3

HOUSTON DYNAMO

Twitter: @HoustonDynamo
First season: 2006
MLS Cup: 2
US Open Cup: 1
Supporters' Shield: 0

Known For
Two MLS Cups
Passionate fans
Dominic Kinnear
Brian Ching
Brad Davis
Pat Onstad
Wade Barrett
DaMarcus Beasley

A BRIEF TEAM HISTORY

After entering the league in 2006, Houston Dynamo—sometimes called the Orange Crush—has done well, winning the MLS Cup twice. A *Houston Chronicle* story laid out some of the meaning behind the Dynamo's name choice. "'*Dynamo* is a word to describe someone who never fatigues, never gives up,' team president Oliver Luck said. 'The new name is symbolic of Houston as an energetic, hard-working, risk-taking kind of town.'"[28] As of 2018, Dynamo owners included Gabriel Brener, Oscar De La Hoya (yes, the former boxer), Ben Guill, and Jake Silverstein.

US OPEN CUP

Houston won its first US Open Cup in 2018 by defeating Philadelphia 3-0 with the help of two goals from Mauro Manotas, and an own goal from Philly.

FACTS ABOUT THEIR CITY

Houston, an oil rich city in Texas, has a population of around 6.3 million people in the greater metro area. Many local beers exist, including 8th Wonder Brewery, Under the Radar Brewery, Saint Arnold Brewing Company, Town in City Brewing Company, and Great Heights Brewing Company. A few supporters' groups that enjoy home games include The Firm (Brickwall), El Batallon, and Texian Army. Great restaurants to pay a visit around Houston include Brennan's of Houston, La Table Houston, The Palm Houston, Hugo's, Kiran's Restaurant, Himalaya Restaurant, Taste of Texas, and Aquarium Restaurant.

WHERE THE TEAM IS TODAY: TACTICS AND STRATEGIES

Tactically speaking, the Dynamo are seeking improvement from the 2018 year. Houston will likely field a 4-2-3-1 formation, or possibly a 4-3-3. It's a team that's looking to utilize the talents of DaMarcus Beasley (a longstanding veteran), Arturo Alvarez, and Tomas Martinez. The Dynamo should provide quick movement down the wings, along with a flurry of skillful midfield combinations in its approach to having a solid 2019 MLS season. Contributions may also come from Mauro Manotas, Andrew Wenger, Alberth Elis, Romell Quioto, Boniek Garcia (a talented player from Honduras), Adam Lundqvist, and Leonardo. As of early September 2018, Houston's Goals For (GF) was 43, while its Goals Against (GA) was 42—pretty close. This is partially why its ranking in the Western Conference was 10th place, with the playoffs right around the corner. (At the same time, FC Dallas, who was in first place in the Western Conference, had a GF of 47, and a GA of 37.) As a team approaching the end of the 2018 season, the September standings were indicative of the tough place Houston found itself in. By season's end, Dynamo finished ninth.

The goal of 2019 would clearly be to widen this gap in favor of GF as the Dynamo look to bring back the sparkling results it has been known for in past championship years.

WILMER CABRERA: A BRIEF COACHING PORTRAIT

Wilmer Cabrera is a former player with national team experience with Colombia. As a defender, he played with a number of professional teams, eventually ending his career with the Long Island Rough Riders. He's had his hands in a number of different coaching assignments, including some time with U17 and U18 US national teams, and Chivas USA. With Wilmer Cabrera, don't be surprised to see a 4-2-3-1 or perhaps a 4-3-3 formation.

KEY PLAYERS AND THEIR CHARACTERISTICS

DaMarcus Beasley, Arturo Alvarez, and Tomas Martinez

DaMarcus Beasley is a speedy outside defender with many years of experience, some of which were spent with Chicago Fire and the USMNT. Over the years, some criticism has fallen on his first touch, but he tends to make up for it with lightning quickness as he's proven to be a tough defender to get past.

With some games under his belt, Arturo Alvarez is a veteran midfielder, having played with numerous sides including the San Jose Earthquakes, Real Salt Lake, and some time spent with El Salvador's national team. Should he stay with Houston, he brings added experience to the table.

Houston has a talented player in Tomas Martinez. The midfielder was born in 1995 and has some experience with the U20 national team of Argentina. It's always good to have a South American on board, and Houston probably wants to hold on to Martinez before another club comes knocking.

KEY PLAYER STATS

(Total career goals with this club)

	Games Played	Goals	Scoring Percentage
DaMarcus Beasley	112	3	2%
Arturo Alvarez	18	0	0%
Tomas Martinez	41	7	17%

WHAT TO WATCH FOR ON TV: HOW BRADLEY, IBRAHIMOVIC, NAGBE, AND OTHERS PLAY

DaMarcus Beasley, Tomas Martinez, and Leonardo (a Brazilian defender) made solid contributions in 2018; expect to see much of the same in 2019. A few other players from 2018 to watch out for in 2019 include Mauro Manotas, Andrew Wenger, Alberth Elis, Romell Quioto, Boniek Garcia (a Dynamo veteran), Adam Lundqvist, Leonardo, Jared Watts, Adolfo Machado, Darwin Ceren, Philippe Senderos, and Alejandro Fuenmayor, along with the sure hands of Joe Willis in goal.

Players that have been on loan that might reappear with Houston include Andrew Wenger, a Pennsylvania native, and keep an eye out for Memo Rodriguez, a younger player from Texas that might become an integral part of the team down the road.

Overall Team Rating: 7.7

LA GALAXY

Twitter: @LAGalaxy
First season: 1996
MLS Cup: 5
US Open Cup: 2
Supporters' Shield: 4

Known For
Being one of the original 10 MLS teams
Five MLS Cups
Passionate and dedicated fans
Bruce Arena
Cobi Jones
David Beckham
Robbie Keane
Landon Donovan
Zlatan Ibrahimovic

A BRIEF TEAM HISTORY

It's the players that make the team tick, and it's the players who will lead the Galaxy to new heights, etching out a place in the history books for this franchise, a bellwether team that is leading American soccer on a path to greatness. A lot rides on each season, and, as the team moves forward by bringing in the right players, keeping attendance up, and attempting to surpass TV-rating expectations, everything is at stake, even for one of the best teams around. Some would argue that staying on top of every little trend is why the Galaxy have remained so good all these years.

As an original team from 1996, the Galaxy have the most MLS Cups, with five. (Also, in 2000, LA Galaxy won the CONCACAF Champions' Cup.) They've turned into the New York Yankees of MLS, winning the most league titles while also attaining the best talent. They turned the world on its axis with the procurement of David Beckham, and the huge payment he received, and most recently they've added Swedish superstar Zlatan Ibrahimovic to their arsenal. Each year they're the team to beat and they only seem to be getting started, with many more years of success likely to come their way.

US OPEN CUP

The Galaxy have won the US Open Cup twice.

FACTS ABOUT THEIR CITY

Los Angeles—the land of movies, TV, music, fashion, and the dreams of millions—has a population of around 13 million people in the greater metro area.

A few local beers made around LA come from Angel City Brewery and Frogtown Brewery. A few restaurants that are near the stadium include Top Shelf Tacos, Rosario's Italian Restaurant, Blue Lotus Vietnamese Cuisine, Delia's Restaurant, and a Starbucks or two.

Ready for home games are the supporters' groups known as the Angel City Brigade, he Galaxians, and LA Riot Squad.

WHERE THE TEAM IS TODAY: TACTICS AND STRATEGIES

Offensively, LA has a vibrant attack down the wings, with thoughtful passing coming from the midfield. There are a lot of talented players with the Galaxy, and when they're clicking on all cylinders, things tend to go in their favor. If the Galaxy can keep their lineup from 2018 in place, there are many weapons available, including the dos Santos brothers, Emmanuel Boateng, Chris Pontius, Sebastian Lletget, Ola Kamara, Ariel Lassiter, and Zlatan Ibrahimovic.

Defensively, Taylor Twellman—former standout forward with New England Revolution turned commentator—pointed out that individual defending (and not tactics) was lacking from time to time in the 2018 season. LA is a team that is top of the list for quality clubs around the league. Should they clean up little defending details here and there, it's a team that can potentially secure its place as the leader in the Western Conference.

DOMINIC KINNEAR: A BRIEF COACHING PORTRAIT

Sigi Schmid—who began coaching LA Galaxy in 2018—has an interesting backstory. He was born in West Germany and eventually played at UCLA. He was later coach of UCLA, and from there he ended up coaching the U20 United States national team, LA Galaxy, Columbus Crew, and Seattle Sounders. He originally coached LA Galaxy from 1999-2004, returning to the Galaxy again from 2017-2018 only to be replaced by Dominic Kinnear in 2018.

Prior to his coaching career, Kinnear was a very talented player that took the field with a number of teams, including the Colorado Rapids, San Jose Clash, and Tampa Bay Mutiny toward the end of his career; he also acquired over 50 caps with the USMNT.

Coach Kinnear has previously coached the Earthquakes and Dynamo. Most recently, he transitioned in 2018 from the role of assistant coach with the Galaxy to running the show.

Is Kinnear inheriting a pompous team of prima donnas that don't want to practice hard? Guys that want to drift by on pure talent? Guys that would rather enjoy the LA nightlife? Possibly.

While he's figuring this all out, don't be surprised to see a 4-4-2 come game time.

KEY PLAYERS AND THEIR CHARACTERISTICS

Zlatan Ibrahimovic, Giovani dos Santos, Sebastian Lletget, and Ashley Cole

Zlatan Ibrahimovic is one of a kind—very arrogant and very talented (proven while playing with Juventus, Inter Milan, Barcelona, and Paris Saint-Germain). As a taller player who stands about 6'5", Ibrahimovic has uncanny skill, and often looks like a futsal player toying with befuddled defenders momentarily stuck in a trance. Add to this his passing vision, which is very good, and his scoring ability, which is top class, and you've got a phenomenal threat around goal.

In his prime, would Zlatan be considered a better player than Josef Martinez and his MLS record-breaking season of 2018? Despite Martinez having a tremendously brilliant year, I think one would have to go with Zlatan. Not because he's bigger (though as a heavier player he would body opponents off the ball successfully), but because he's a better passer; at times his vision and touch could be mistaken for Platini, though I wouldn't be too quick to throw him in that upper-echelon category as yet. (Many great players are good passers; Rooney's a good passer, but he's not Platini. Platini, Ronaldinho, and Valderrama are in a class all their own.) And Zlatan, in his prime, had a presence that might be more beneficial on the field than Martinez. But such a debate is neither here nor there. Both are brilliant players.

Despite having a knee injury, Zlatan is still capable of greatness for a few more years. However, there is a question as to whether or not he will remain with LA. Writing for *NBC Sports* in 2018, Joe Prince-Wright speculated on a few places that Zlatan might land, including D.C. United, New York City FC, Minnesota United, and Los Angeles FC. Prince-Wright pointed out that all we know is that "Zlatan will be a man in demand if he decides to leave LA over this offseason. But what is more than likely happening here is that Ibrahimovic wants a vastly improved contract to remain in LA beyond the end of his current deal which runs out in December 2019. The Galaxy would be misguided to do anything but offer Zlatan what he wants."[29]

Giovani dos Santos is a very skillful attacking player with a good amount of experience, including stops at Barcelona and Tottenham, and he's well known by American fans as being a member of the Mexican national team. With a quick change of pace, he has the ability to dazzle defenders with elusive dribbling, sometimes going inside toward the middle where he is very effective at causing danger around his opponent's box.

Sebastian Lletget—a midfielder from San Francisco, California—is a player with skill, technique, and good soccer IQ. His presence on the field should help carry the Galaxy in a good direction for the 2019 season and beyond.

Ashley Cole—a longtime member of England's national team—brings an added touch of class to outside defense (and he can also serve as an outside mid). He has great touch on the ball, immaculate technique, and, as a one-on-one defender, he has good speed to close down an opponent's attempt at dribbling down the line.

KEY PLAYER STATS

(Total career goals with this club)

	Games Played	Goals	Scoring Percentage
Zlatan Ibrahimovic	27	22	81%
Giovani dos Santos	77	26	33%
Sebastian Lletget	82	11	13%
Ashley Cole	86	3	3%

WHAT TO WATCH FOR ON TV: HOW BRADLEY, IBRAHIMOVIC, NAGBE, AND OTHERS PLAY

Based on past success and player recruitment, every time LA Galaxy steps on the field there's an expectation to win.

The Galaxy has an arsenal of talent just waiting to overwhelm and bewilder opposing defenses. Emmanuel Boateng will give defenders plenty of trouble down the wings, with bursts of speed, while Ibrahimovic is ever dangerous in the attack with vision, field awareness, a deft touch, cultured passes, and goals. Then, if you're another team weighing your options, you have to contend with the crafty dos Santos brothers, Chris Pontius, Sebastian Lletget, Perry Kitchen, and Ashley Cole, who has a few games under his belt with England. These were featured players in 2018 and Galaxy fans will likely want them to hang around. It's a tough group to contend with, one that has sound players across the board, who are technically gifted and possess a strong awareness of organizational soccer, with the ability to break down an opposing team's strategy.

LA is always a team to reckon with, there's no doubt about that; but the Galaxy didn't have the best year in 2018—by its own standards, anyway. Little things here and there needed improving. For example, during August of 2018, as MLS playoffs were growing near, Kevin Baxter of the *Los Angeles Times* wrote: "The Galaxy have made a bad situation worse by giving up the tying or losing goal in the 82nd minute or later in each of their last three games. Take away those goals and the Galaxy would be atop the conference standings."[30]

Again, as Taylor Twellman pointed out, in 2018, LA was a team that needed to fix individual defending errors.

Possibly the players are lackadaisical, relying on pure talent to get by, happy with minimal effort as they sit back and enjoy the LA lifestyle. That could be the case. If it is, this could be a self-destructive situation holding the Galaxy back from its true potential.

However, with that said, should LA's lineup from 2018 remain in place (or very close to what it was), it's a very gifted team that will almost certainly be one of the top five in the Western Conference during 2019. It's really about how much effort they want to put forward.

Overall Team Rating: 9.1

LOS ANGELES FC

Twitter: @LAFC
First season: 2018
MLS Cup: 0
US Open Cup: 0
Supporters' Shield: 0

Known For
Passionate fans
Bringing a dynamic energy to the league
Bob Bradley
Carlos Vela
Benny Feilhaber
Lee Nguyen
Mia Hamm
Magic Johnson
Tony Robbins
Will Ferrell

A BRIEF TEAM HISTORY

Los Angeles FC is a team with many owners—Mia Hamm, Magic Johnson, Tony Robbins, and Will Ferrell, to name a few—and the introduction of LAFC has given American soccer another exciting franchise, while also creating a cross-town rivalry with the Galaxy. In 2018—LAFC's very first season—this rivalry quickly became surrounded with controversy. Writing for the *Los Angeles Times*, Kevin Baxter reported that "six fans were arrested and 14 ejected from Bank of California Stadium during Thursday's MLS soccer game between the Galaxy and the Los Angeles Football Club."

"LAFC said it had doubled security at its stadium for the game—the second in the expansion team's intracity rivalry with the Galaxy but the first in its new Exposition Park home—but clashes between fans of the two teams began outside the venue about two hours before kickoff, with video posted to social media showing a group of men dressed in black and red LAFC jerseys physically attacking two people in white Galaxy jerseys.

"Supporters of both teams also clashed inside the stadium while uniformed officers from the LAPD and California Highway Patrol broke up fights as fans left the game. In addition, 78 seats in an upper-deck corner section reserved for Galaxy fans were either damaged or ripped out."[31] While violence isn't productive for the future of the league, LAFC and the Galaxy definitely have a rivalry at hand.

Aside from its showdown with the Galaxy, during the 2018 season, LAFC was part of an ongoing conversation—and an uplifting one, at that—revolving around other expansion teams, including Miami, Nashville, and Cincinnati. If anything, the addition of LAFC served as motivation to other investors around the country eager to galvanize an MLS franchise in their city. The introduction of Los Angeles FC was proof yet again that MLS was alive and well and expanding.

US OPEN CUP

To date, Los Angeles FC has not won the US Open Cup, but it's a very new team, and this may change soon.

FACTS ABOUT THEIR CITY

LA has a population of around 13 million people in the greater metro area. LA has a vibrant college sports history, particularly with USC (which has produced many Heisman Trophy winners) and UCLA (which has the legendary basketball program made famous by John Wooden, along with an excellent soccer team).

As of 2016, the Los Angeles Rams are back, making a new start in LA after a long stay in St. Louis. The return of the Rams, along with LAFC's arrival, has provided a buzz of new energy to LA. Currently, in the greater LA area, there are two NBA teams, two MLS teams, two MLB teams, and two NHL teams, along with an NFL team. Not bad!

Los Angeles might not be known as the beer capitol of the country, but there are interesting beers produced there, which might surprise a few people. Some local beer around LA that fans might enjoy comes from Boomtown Brewery and Highland Park Brewery, to name a couple.

WHERE THE TEAM IS TODAY: TACTICS AND STRATEGIES

Offensively, under the coaching of Bob Bradley, LAFC is considered a team that delivers death by possession to its opponents. Possession is good; a lot of possession is even better. Over the years, many critics of MLS have asserted that it's a league without proper possession. The fact that Bradley is presenting a team that values possession is a good thing. The 2018 MLS season featured many talented LAFC players that could pull off impressive stints of possession, including Benny Feilhaber, Lee Nguyen, and Carlos Vela, to name a few. Feilhaber and Nguyen have a vibe about them that is a little reminiscent of FC Barcelona from 2008-2012. Feilhaber and Nguyen need the right coach and system to excel; and they need their teammates to believe in the system—everyone needs to be all-in and on the same page. Obviously, Feilhaber and Nguyen aren't exactly pulling off possession at a Barcelona level, but there's something there, and those two players have that capability within them, which, with a little fine-tuning, will be a great asset for LAFC.

Sometimes, the best defense is a good offense. If this is the case, LAFC has a good start. Defensively speaking, Jordan Harvey, Walker Zimmerman, Danilo Silva (who was on loan), Joao Moutinho, and Dejan Jakovic all played a role in 2018, which turned out to be a successful season. It will be interesting to see how they pan out during 2019 and beyond.

BOB BRADLEY: A BRIEF COACHING PORTRAIT

Bob Bradley has a very experienced and accomplished coaching resume. He's led an impressive list of teams, some of which include Princeton University, Chicago Fire, New York/New Jersey MetroStars, the USMNT, Egypt, Swansea City, and now LAFC.

Under Bradley, the USMNT placed second at the 2009 FIFA Confederations Cup in South Africa, and during the 2010 World Cup, Bradley led the team on an exciting run that included a late-game victory against Algeria.

One of Bradley's most challenging jobs as a coach has to have been his brave attempt to steer Swansea City in the right direction. Many British people have little respect for Americans when it comes to soccer, so for Bradley to have won that city over completely, his team would need to have won each game by a score of 6-0, and even then there probably would've been calls for him to leave town. "Not good enough!" they'd call out. "You call that coaching?!" Now Bradley has found a home in LA, and during his first season things went very well.

Don't be surprised to see a 4-3-3 formation as LAFC moves forward under Bradley's direction, and expect to see a strong emphasis on tactical passing with a constructive approach to possession soccer.

KEY PLAYERS AND THEIR CHARACTERISTICS

Carlos Vela, Diego Rossi, Benny Feilhaber, and Lee Nguyen

Carlos Vela is an experienced player, one that has played many games with the Mexican national team, representing his country in the 2018 World Cup and scoring a goal against South Korea. (Despite having a good showing in the group stage, which was highlighted with a victory over Germany, it was yet another World Cup that ended in the second round for Mexico.) As an attacking player, Vela has skillful touch, good awareness on the field, and the international experience that should serve LAFC well on its quest to win the MLS Cup.

Born in 1998, young Diego Rossi brings a skillful, cultured Uruguayan touch to the attack. Keep an eye out for good things from him.

Brazilion-born Benny Feilhaber is an experienced USMNT midfielder that arrived in LA after a stay with Sporting Kansas City. Once a member of the UCLA Bruins, Feilhaber's back in LA looking to make a difference. He specializes in possession soccer and skillful passing. Watch for him distributing the ball between the defenders and forwards, with the intent of achieving harmony between the two.

Lee Nguyen has some USMNT experience—a little less than he deserves, actually—but given that he's entering his early thirties, that boat may have sailed. He's had an interesting professional career, however, playing with a handful of teams, including

PSV; Randers FC (in Denmark); two Vietnamese clubs, Hoang Anh Gia Lai FC, and Becamex Binh Duong FC; New England Revolution; and now he's landed with LAFC. At New England, Nguyen took the league by storm and, at one time, was considered one of the best players in Major League Soccer; he was an MVP contender in 2014. As things stand today, he definitely is one of the top players in MLS, but not necessarily an MVP candidate. He is a great player with high-level passing ability, dribbling prowess, and a special ability to break down a defense with in-the-moment quality; he's a player that always seems to find an opening whether it's a pass or dribble, and he adds a ton of value to LA's offense.

KEY PLAYER STATS

(Total career goals with this club)

	Games Played	Goals	Scoring Percentage
Carlos Vela	28	14	50%
Diego Rossi	32	12	37%
Benny Feilhaber	34	3	8%
Lee Nguyen	25	3	12%

WHAT TO WATCH FOR ON TV: HOW BRADLEY, IBRAHIMOVIC, NAGBE, AND OTHERS PLAY

Coach Bradley can be seen on the sideline with an intent stare, one that is totally focused on the task at hand while also subtly propagating the idealistic aura of someone to be taken seriously, a true student of the game, and someone that might just see each game as a microcosm of how he believes the USMNT can someday win the World Cup. While winning the World Cup may be a personal quest of Bradley's, he now has his eyes set on dominating MLS again, to relive some of his glory days from Chicago. Who says it can't be done? Bradley's completely saddled up and ready for the challenge. What better place for this to happen than in LA?

The fantastic, wheeling and dealing, no holds barred Los Angeles FC. One of MLS's newest success stories, they wear the gold, black, and white jerseys. LAFC can dazzle you with skill, tough defense, and optimism as a new team in the league determined to make a name for itself. Beside the high-profile ownership group, it seems like a team intent on proving the investors right. It's also a team invested in creating a winning program for the dedicated fans. With each touch of the ball, LAFC is a club that seems to know its place in history; for now, we'll wait and see the ending.

As a new team, LAFC is in a grace period, wherein the organization needs a winning record to ensure people are sitting in seats; however, as a brand-new team there's a window of time where it's okay to meet low expectations, and it's certainly okay to meet high expectations. Why? Because it has no track record to go with (aside from its one and only season). On the flip side, LA Galaxy is in a situation where it has to meet high expectations all the time, because it's an organization that has already achieved so much, and, as is often the case, getting anything less than the MLS Cup trophy is unacceptable to fans and leaders within the organization. Therefore, for a team in LAFC's current position—a group waltzing into its second season—everything's okay, and, thus, it's a team that can get away with having fun, while approaching each game with a professional attitude. It's an added bonus when your offensive frontline includes the ball-handling capability of Vela, Nguyen, and Feilhaber. If these three standout players remain with the team throughout 2019, it should be a recipe for fluid, exciting, and fun soccer to watch.

Overall Team Rating: 9.3

MINNESOTA UNITED FC

Twitter: @MNUFC
First season: 2017
MLS Cup: 0
US Open Cup: 0
Supporters' Shield: 0

Known For
Passionate fans
Being an expansion team
Enriching the league and growing soccer in the northern US
Adrian Heath
Miguel Ibarra
Ibson

A BRIEF TEAM HISTORY

Minnesota United FC played its first MLS game in 2017. United FC's home games are played in TCF Bank Stadium, in Minneapolis, though Allianz Field stadium, in Saint Paul, will likely be its next destination, kicking off in the 2019 season.

While Minnesota is a team without any major trophies yet, they're on the move, looking to advance to the top position within MLS. As an expansion team, this is a strong challenge, but for now, for the most part, people in Minnesota are very excited about the team and the revenue it will add to the local economy.

Soccer in Minnesota has always been prevalent to residents of the north, with ups and downs, quality and optimism. Currently, a big concern for American soccer is the expansion of the game into more US cities, thus broadening MLS. Minneapolis-Saint Paul is one such place that has recently received more attention as MLS has embraced Minnesota into its league.

Back in December of 2015, the matter of building a soccer-specific stadium was under review, as Saint Paul mayor Chris Coleman was rumored to be supporting construction of the stadium in Saint Paul with property tax exemption, working with the state of Minnesota to allow a sales tax exemption for construction materials, according to a story written on July 13, 2015 by Eric Boehm, at Watchdog.org.[32] Views from local businesses varied, however. Julia, a manager at Golden Fig Fine Foods in Saint Paul said, "It'll bring people to Saint Paul, so that's an added bonus."* This is the hope of any expansion team—to expand the reach of their brand while creating excitement for local businesses. It's the technical process of building a stadium that had some residents up in arms. An anonymous business owner commented, "I'm against public subsidies of any sports stadiums," adding sarcastically, "My business is in a mall and

---

*   From a phone interview on 12-16-15.

it's getting old—shouldn't the public pay for renovations to my building as well?"†

William McGuire, of the Minnesota United, and Mayor Coleman view the arrival of the team as a great asset to the community, one which will yield profits to surrounding business owners for years to come.

Minnesota is not unfamiliar with a professional soccer franchise. From 2010 to the present, the Minnesota United FC competed in the NASL, before MLS announced expansion intentions in March of 2015. Prior to that (during some of Pelé's 1975-1977 tour) were the Minnesota Kicks, who played in the NASL from 1976 through 1981, and hosted games at Metropolitan Stadium in Bloomington, Minnesota. Back then, commissioner Phil Woosnam was overly optimistic that American soccer would grow on a steady path, which unfortunately did not come true until the inception of MLS in 1996. Reasons included some competition from professional indoor soccer (Major Indoor Soccer League) which began in 1978, and the lack of soccer-specific stadiums; it was difficult for soccer to take off as some games were played on football fields, or baseball diamonds, which never provided the game a true identity.

Things are changing fast as MLS continues to branch out and a lot of a potential rests in American soccer, embraced by great cities like Minneapolis-Saint Paul.

---

†   From a phone interview on 12-16-15.

US OPEN CUP

To date, Minnesota United FC has not won the US Open Cup.

FACTS ABOUT THEIR CITY

Minneapolis–Saint Paul has a population of around 3.1 million people in the urban area.

Dangerous Man Brewing Company, Indeed Brewing Company, and Taproom are local beers that fans might enjoy around game time. Minneapolis restaurants include Spoon and Stable, Bar La Grassa, and many others; should someone visit any of these, they're sure to be in good hands, Midwest style.

Check out Minnesota United's supporters' groups that go by Dark Clouds and True North Elite.

WHERE THE TEAM IS TODAY: TACTICS AND STRATEGIES

As for the 2018 season, it was not the best year for Minnesota, but neither was it the worst one. Call it a learning experience. Come 2019, Minnesota is looking to re-boot its game plan, and there is plenty of optimism afoot.

Offensively, Miguel Ibarra and Ibson provide a glimpse of hope up front, while on the defensive end, Francisco Calvo, Brent Kallman, and Michael Boxall made contributions in 2018.

Should they remain with the team, watch for their leadership on the backline as they protect the goal for goalkeeper Bobby Shuttleworth.

Coach Adrian Heath should likely have these players working in tandem with potentially different formations, though this is yet to be seen. Sometimes, when the previous season wasn't one to write home about, a lot of tinkering can result. Minnesota's quest for greatness should have a lot to do with Heath's approach throughout the year, which may have some different configurations.

ADRIAN HEATH: A BRIEF COACHING PORTRAIT

Adrian Heath was born in England and played professionally with a number of teams, some of which included Everton and Manchester City.

Are formations important? Are they sometimes confusing? The late coach, Brian Clough, didn't think much of them, that's for sure. According to Clough, what mattered was how the players played and whether or not they felt comfortable within their role on the field. As for Heath, don't be surprised to see a 3-1-4-2 formation (essentially a 4-4-2), a 3-5-2, or even a 3-4-1-2 (which might as well be a 3-5-2) as he leads Minnesota United into what has the potential to be a brilliant season.

KEY PLAYERS AND THEIR CHARACTERISTICS

Miguel Ibarra and Ibson

Miguel Ibarra is a midfielder from the US that has some experience on the USMNT. He will likely be a vital component in this upcoming season for Minnesota, and beyond.

Ibson was born in Brazil. That's always a good start. As a midfielder, he's played for a handful of teams before Minnesota, including Flamengo and Corinthians. As the season progresses—should Ibson stay with Minnesota—watch for him distributing the ball with a nuanced South American touch.

KEY PLAYER STATS

(Total career goals with this club)

	Games Played	Goals	Scoring Percentage
Miguel Ibarra	62	10	16%
Ibson	58	4	6%

WHAT TO WATCH FOR ON TV: HOW BRADLEY, IBRAHIMOVIC, NAGBE, AND OTHERS PLAY

While you've had Ibson and Miguel Ibarra leading the charge up front, a few other featured players from 2018 included Mason Toye, Angelo Rodriguez, Rasmus Schuller, Eric Miller, Collen Warner, Collin Martin, Frantz Pangop, Francisco Calvo, Brent Kallman, Michael Boxall, and Bobby Shuttleworth. Should this unit stay in place, Minnesota has a firm grip for the future, though don't be surprised to see players move around in order to find the right chemistry.

Minnesota plays all out in an attempt to bring home a championship. Team unity is the mantra that appears to loom overhead as Minnesota entertains its fans on the field. Keep an eye out for this to continue throughout the 2019 season, as Minnesota will probably go with a 3-1-4-2 formation (which is essentially a 4-4-2). With that said, I predict that there is close to a zero chance that Minnesota will win the 2019 MLS Cup. It's a young franchise and, unlike Atlanta United FC (also a young franchise), there just isn't enough tantalizing talent across the board to put Minnesota over the top. However, it's a team on the rise with something to prove and that should make for an interesting season—and possibly a Cinderella season at that!

Overall Team Rating: 7.1

PORTLAND TIMBERS

Twitter: @TimbersFC
First season: 2011
MLS Cup: 1
US Open Cup: 0
Supporters' Shield: 0

Known For
Winning the MLS Cup
Sellout games
Insanely loud fans
Insanely passionate fans
Caleb Porter
Darlington Nagbe
Diego Valeri
Deforestation every time a goal is scored*

---

*   Every time a goal is scored, the team mascot slices off part of a log
     with a chainsaw and the piece of wood represents the goal scored.

A BRIEF TEAM HISTORY

The first MLS game for the amazing Timbers was in 2011 in front of a community of fans that are intensely passionate about their soccer.

Caleb Porter—a native of Tacoma, Washington, and a former Indiana University standout—led the team as coach from 2013-2017, earning an MLS Cup championship title for the team and city of Portland in the process. To date, this is the first and only MLS Cup for the Timbers.

For the 2018 season, Giovanni Savarese started his run as head coach of the Timbers. Porter was gone, and so too was the maestro on the midfield, Darlington Nagbe. In their absence, under the guidance of Savarese, the Timbers did a good job remaining very competitive throughout the 2018 season. For a club still under ten years in the league, it has accomplished a lot, with fans that keep the drumbeat going strong.

US OPEN CUP

To date, the Timbers have not won the US Open Cup.

FACTS ABOUT THEIR CITY

Portland has a population of around 2.3 million people in the greater metro area. Of that population, there's a passionate group of soccer-goers, to say the least.

Who has the best fans? This is an oft-asked question, and the answer really comes down to opinion; it seems as though every player in the history of sports insists that their fans are the best. However, it's really hard for me to say that any other MLS fan base can outperform that of Portland and their main rival, Seattle. Home games in these cities are a unique experience, including Portland's "Timber Joey."

Timber Joey is a fixture in games, a man dressed up like a lumberjack, waiting calmly—some might say desperately—for a home goal so that he can do what he does best: carve a piece of wood from a tree trunk with a chainsaw as the crowd goes wild! It's a symbolic act unique to the Portland Timbers, speaking directly to the historic legacy of lumberjacks in the Northwest, a profession embraced by manly men, men eager to drink beer after a long day's work of risking their lives around large falling trees. Ironically, Timber Joey represents a historic profession that many in the area are proud of while simultaneously offending the liberal crowd of Portland who are undoubtedly questioning Timber Joey's symbolic act and its effect on the environment. Regardless, for most fans, it's pretty cool to see a tree carved up when there is a goal.

Timbers Army is the supporters' group strutting its stuff at home games, making as much noise as possible.

Portland offers many local beers including—but definitely not limited to—Base Camp Brewing Company, Culmination Brewing, Upright Brewing, 10 Barrel Brewing, Bridgeport Brewing Company, and Old Town Brewing. It's an area that loves its beer, along with the local soccer team.

Restaurants around town include Toro Bravo, Imperial, Bamboo Sushi, and Gracie's Restaurant. Kaitlin Dover, general manager at Gracie's Restaurant, said the Alaskan salmon is one of their well-known dishes. She added that The 19th Hole (which houses a beer garden) is also a popular destination.

WHERE THE TEAM IS TODAY: TACTICS AND STRATEGIES

Offensively, Portland uses a flurry of passes and daring attempts around goal, while, defensively, it's a team that has athletic stoppers at virtually every position, making it hard for opposition forces to attain good scoring chances on goal. Portland will likely field a 4-3-3 or possibly a 4-3-2-1 formation.

GIOVANNI SAVARESE: A BRIEF COACHING PORTRAIT

Giovanni Savarese is a coach from Venezuela that has a lot to prove as Caleb Porter's replacement. An MLS Cup championship would be a good start. That's the goal for any coach, and, in Savarese's case, he's replacing a coach that summited that mountaintop.

Savarese played for New England Revolution, along with a host of other teams during his playing days. As a former forward, many would argue that's just the experience that a head coach needs in order to guide a team like Portland—one that embraces skill over brute force—to the top of the Western Conference.

KEY PLAYERS AND THEIR CHARACTERISTICS

Diego Valeri and Sebastian Blanco

Born in Argentina, Diego Valeri won the 2017 MLS MVP award. His resume includes playing in the most recent 2018 MLS All-Star game, and suiting up with the Argentinian national team. While he's not a crafty dribbling type, he's a threat around goal in the style of Robert Lewandowski of Poland. Valeri is a very talented scorer that places himself in good positions to utilize his well-crafted finishing technique. Watch for his offensive expertise in the 2019 season as the Timbers look to stay in contention for the MLS Cup.

Sebastian Blanco was born in Argentina, and as a midfielder he's shuffled around with a few teams, eventually landing at Portland. He brings experience with the Argentinian national team to the table.

KEY PLAYER STATS

(Total career goals with this club)

	Games Played	Goals	Scoring Percentage
Diego Valeri	180	68	37%
Sebastian Blanco	64	18	28%

WHAT TO WATCH FOR ON TV: HOW BRADLEY, IBRAHIMOVIC, NAGBE, AND OTHERS PLAY

Portland is led up front by Valeri, who has a great presence around goal and who is surrounded by brilliant passers and auxiliary forces in the attack, such as Blanco. Dairon Asprilla, Andy Polo (who was on loan), Cristhian Paredes (who was on loan), Zarek Valentin, Julio Cascante, and veteran midfielder Diego Chara played important roles in the 2018 season, so keep an eye out for them potentially doing the same in 2019. Also watch for new additions throughout the year, which may be pivotal for the team's direction. As it stands, it's a club that will overwhelm opponents with skill, flurries of passes, and the twelfth man—the enormously powerful fan base that comes to life like a sonic boom during home games.

Overall Team Rating: 8.9

REAL SALT LAKE

Twitter: @RealSaltLake
First season: 2005
MLS Cup: 1
US Open Cup: 0
Supporters' Shield: 0

Known For
Winning the MLS Cup
Dedicated fans
Jason Kreis
Clint Mathis
Eddie Pope
Kyle Beckerman

A BRIEF TEAM HISTORY

Real Salt Lake has one MLS Cup championship from 2009, a great accomplishment considering the competition. Currently, the franchise is searching for that past magic, looking for a repeat as champions. It's a small-market team whose first MLS season was in 2005. Back then John Ellinger—a native of Baltimore, Maryland—was head coach.

There have been great names walking through the doors, including Jason Kreis, Eddie Pope, and Clint Mathis, to name a few. Along Real Salt Lake's journey, which is of middle age in terms of MLS criteria, one player in particular has been with the franchise for many, many years: Kyle Beckerman. Now close to finishing his professional career, he's seen about everything a player can during his time at Real. He was there for the glory days, and he's provided leadership for upcoming players within the program; one thing he stresses is winning. Under his guidance, Real won just enough to sneak into the 2018 MLS Cup Playoffs.

As of 2018, the team owner was Dell Loy Hansen, with Mike Petke as the head coach. Heading into 2019, Petke (alongside veteran midfielder Beckerman) looks to make history as he leads the team toward what Real Salt Lake fans hope to be a winning season, followed by another MLS Cup title, and, possibly a repeat thumping of rival Colorado Rapids like the classic 6-0 victory from August 25, 2018.

US OPEN CUP

To this date, Real Salt Lake has not won a US Open Cup, though, in their defense, they do have one MLS Cup under their belt, which they would probably prefer.

FACTS ABOUT THEIR CITY

Salt Lake City is located in the great state of Utah and it has a population of around 1.1 million people in the greater metro area.

If you're a fan of beer and you want something local, you might want to try Epic Brewing Company. Awesome restaurants to check out around Salt Lake City include The Roof, Aristo's Greek Restaurant, and Eva, among others.

Supporters' groups include La Barra Real, Riot Brigade, Rogue Cavaliers Brigade, Royal Army, Salt City United, and Section 26.

WHERE THE TEAM IS TODAY: TACTICS AND STRATEGIES

Defensively, this is a team that'll likely field a 4-2-3-1 formation. Offensively, this is a younger team. From a 2018 story in *The Salt Lake Tribune*, Christopher Kamrani wrote: "This isn't like the RSL rosters of the glory years. This team is replete with players in their early 20s, academy products or international rising stars trying to establish themselves in MLS and perhaps beyond."[33] As the 2019 season winds on, watch for this team to grow in experience and confidence.

MIKE PETKE: A BRIEF COACHING PORTRAIT

Mike Petke—a native of New York state—was a defender during his playing years with a few MLS teams, eventually finishing up his career with the New York Red Bulls. He also coached the Red Bulls for a time, before landing in Salt Lake.

From a May 2018 story in *The Salt Lake Tribune*, Maddie Lee captured a glimpse of Petke's approach: "RSL was about two weeks into an experiment Mike Petke had launched after a 3-1 loss at Toronto. He put a different player in charge of the first half of warm-ups every day in an effort to bring out personalities and encourage leadership. Between that and continuous conversations with individuals and the group on the subject, Petke said he's seen players respond by being more vocal."[34] At first glance, this might seem like a superfluous gesture, yet it strikes at the heart of most athletic teams. In fact, much of the on-field cohesion has to do with off-field chemistry. While Petke works on this aspect of bringing his team together, he'll likely send his troops onto the field in a 4-2-3-1 formation, which, in the eyes of some, provides balance in the middle of the field, allowing the players to work their magic.

KEY PLAYERS AND THEIR CHARACTERISTICS

Kyle Beckerman and Joao Plata

Kyle Beckerman is an interesting player. The best compliment available for Beckerman is this: Once he bores you to death, you realize his steadiness is his best attribute. His qualities reside in his ability to lead and to provide structure, along with safe passes that keep the heartbeat of the team moving in a positive direction.

Not only does Beckerman add steadiness in the central midfield area, he also provides a great deal of experience. As a veteran in the latter half of his career—one that has included numerous USMNT games—Beckerman has attained the tools necessary from his vast and expansive experience to lead Real Salt Lake in the right direction. From a 2018 story in *The Salt Lake Tribune*, Christopher Kamrani highlighted some of Beckerman's attributes and accomplishments: "Beckerman remains the club's captain, the voice that radiates throughout pregame huddles and daily training sessions. He's the guy who can still make the game look pretty when necessary, and who can muck it up when it's called for, too. He's the owner of some of the most time-tested records in Major League Soccer history; no field player has ever started more matches (420) or played more minutes (37,582) than Beckerman."[35] Kyle will definitely go down as a great fixture in the history of the league.

Joao Plata is an attacking player from Ecuador who has played a few games for his national team. He's been with Real Salt Lake since 2013, with over 140 games played. Keep an eye on Plata as he works his way through defenses.

KEY PLAYER STATS

(Total career goals with this club)

	Games Played	Goals	Scoring Percentage
Kyle Beckerman	315	30	9%
Joao Plata	158	45	28%

WHAT TO WATCH FOR ON TV: HOW BRADLEY, IBRAHIMOVIC, NAGBE, AND OTHERS PLAY

If Real Salt Lake can keep its 2018 roster in place—which is a challenge for many teams—there's a chance of maintaining the level of competition needed to compete for the top position in the Western Conference. Some players from 2018 that may return for the 2019 campaign are Corey Baird, Sesbastian Saucedo, Joao Plata, Jefferson Savarino, Albert Rusnak, Stephen Sunday, Damir Kreilach, Danny Acosta, Justen Glad, Marcelo Silva, Brooks Lennon, Aaron Herrera, and the experienced goalkeeper with a number of games representing the USMNT, Nick Rimando. Real Salt Lake will hope to have steady contributions from Beckerman and Plata, as this is a team with resolve and determination, one that's looking to recapture the MLS Cup.

Overall Team Rating: 8

SAN JOSE EARTHQUAKES

Twitter: @SJEarthquakes
First season: 1996
MLS Cup: 2
US Open Cup: 0
Supporters' Shield: 2

Known For
Being one of the original 10 MLS teams
Two MLS Cups
A strong fan base
Eric Wynalda
Eddie Lewis
Troy Dayak
Landon Donovan
Brian Ching
Dwayne De Rosario
Jeff Agoos
Wade Barrett
Chris Wondolowski

A BRIEF TEAM HISTORY

The San Jose Earthquakes (previously known as the San Jose Clash) are one of the original teams in MLS. It had a very good run of success with Landon Donovan, before he moved on to play with the Galaxy. Donovan—who went on to be the all-time MLS scoring leader with 145—got many of his early goals playing for San Jose.

With two MLS Cups in its trophy case, the Earthquakes have been led more recently by Chris Wondolowski. At the close of the 2018 MLS season, Wondolowski—a prolific scorer—came close to surpassing Landon Donovan's all-time league scoring record as he tallied up 144 career goals. Overall, San Jose has won the Supporters' Shield twice, along with two MLS Cups.

US OPEN CUP

To date, despite having success with the MLS Cup, the Earthquakes have not won a US Open Cup.

FACTS ABOUT THEIR CITY

San Jose has a population of around 1.9 million people in the greater metro area. The Bay Area is known more for wine than beer, and when I owned a restaurant in the North Bay (a little Thai and California cuisine fusion restaurant called Thai Ginger Bistro), I would tell tourists to visit the Silverado Trail in Napa, a road that borders the main highway of wineries there. This may be a bit of a drive, but it's worth it. The North Bay is considered by most people to be the wine capital of the world, along with wineries in Sonoma, Healdsburg, and other various locations scattered around the bay and extending into the South Bay, closer to where the Earthquakes play. Should travelers find their way up north into Sonoma County and the historic downtown of Petaluma, my previous business neighbor, Jason Jenkins— owner of Vine & Barrel Wines and a true wine and culture connoisseur—is still in business, with wine tasting and snacks available.

Restaurant options closer to Avaya Stadium include Ramen Taka, Annie's Sandwiches, Crepes Bistro, and the always busy In-N-Out Burger. As far as beer goes, the San Jose area has a few options, including Santa Clara Valley Brewing and Lazy Duck Brewing.

Within the South Bay area are some multi-million-dollar teams, including the Oakland A's, San Francisco Giants, Oakland Raiders, San Francisco 49ers, Golden State Warriors, San Jose Sharks, and the San Jose Earthquakes, who operate out of Avaya Stadium which holds 18,000 people. Supporting the Earthquakes on their quest for greatness are the supporter's groups known as San Jose Ultras, The Casbah, and The Faultline.

WHERE THE TEAM IS TODAY: TACTICS AND STRATEGIES

According to Jake Pisani, communications manager of the San Jose Earthquakes, they have been putting a lot of resources into their youth academy. The academy teams play home games in San Jose and train in Sunnyvale. Although a few MLS academies have residency programs, San Jose's academy players commute. There is a rich talent pool in the Bay Area, and the club is expecting a lot of progress down the road.

Offensively, with very few wins from the 2018 season, San Jose is a team trying to find its groove. The formation will likely be a 4-4-2, which allows Chris Wondolowski—the team's top scorer—to post up top, receive passes, and contribute to the flow of possession, while establishing himself in smart positions around the box to increase his scoring chances (something he does very well). In 2018, Wondolowski was paired up front with Danny Hoesen, and if the Dutch-born striker remains in San Jose, there's a potent attack brewing with the two of them.

Defensively, coming off a losing season, the Earthquakes have a lot of adjustments to make. In terms of moving forward, sometimes it's best to keep a short memory, regain confidence, and look to improve upon little things on the field, such as one-on-one defending, anticipating tackles, and group shape. Almost certainly, these points will be on the minds of the players throughout 2019.

MATIAS ALMEYDA: A BRIEF COACHING PORTRAIT

In 2018, Swedish-born coach Mikael Stahre was replaced by Steve Ralston. Ralston is a St. Louis product who holds the second-highest all-time record of assists, right behind Landon

Donovan. For a team that was lurking around the bottom of the Western Conference in 2018, it's a difficult task for the coach to solely turn things around, and it's often an easy decision to replace a coach, appeasing fans and allowing them to feel as though something better will result. As of October 1, 2018, an inside source said that Ralston was an interim head coach, and a replacement would likely be named in late 2018 or early 2019.

Indeed, prior to 2019, the Earthquakes named Matias Almeyda as the new coach. Almeyda, who played with Argentina's national team, will bring a South American touch to the team. This might end up being a great turning point for the franchise. One thing is certain: Almeyda will be looking to stage an epic comeback during the 2019 season. Whether or not such a thing can be achieved, for better or worse, the coach usually takes the majority of blame. It's a difficult task to take a team that finished last in 2018 and turn everything around overnight. Don't be surprised to see a 4-4-2 formation, which would be the safest bet for a new coach—or even another coaching change. Regardless, an interesting storyline is building in San Jose: Can the right coach be found to get the franchise out of last place?

KEY PLAYERS AND THEIR CHARACTERISTICS

Chris Wondolowski and Danny Hoesen

Chris Wondolowski is the type of forward that every other forward is jealous of. Quite simply, the ball just seems to gravitate toward him in the box. Somehow, he's in the right place at the right time—a lot. Back in 2012, the prolific scorer tied the MLS league record—originally set by Roy Lassiter in 1996—for goals scored in a single season with 27. Tying this record established Wondolowski as a top forward, one of the league's best. He brings passion to the field, along with plenty of experience from his time with the USMNT. He's not the fastest or quickest guy around, but he definitely has good technique and a unique ability to find the back of the net.

Danny Hoesen is a forward from Holland with experience from the Dutch youth national team levels. Should he stay with the Earthquakes, watch for him to combine up top with Wondolowski to put points on the board, and push the team into the 2019 MLS Playoffs.

KEY PLAYER STATS

(Total career goals with this club)

	Games Played	Goals	Scoring Percentage
Chris Wondolowski	290	140	48%
Danny Hoesen	66	17	25%

WHAT TO WATCH FOR ON TV: HOW BRADLEY, IBRAHIMOVIC, NAGBE, AND OTHERS PLAY

With two MLS cups under its belt, San Jose is a franchise that belongs to an elite club that includes Sporting Kansas City, Houston Dynamo, D.C. United, and LA Galaxy; however, at times, it feels like the Earthquakes are nowhere to be seen. This might just be the impetus it needs to stage a fierce campaign in the 2019 MLS season.

A few players that were featured in 2018 include Vako Qazaishvili, Anibal Godoy, Florian Jungwirth, Fatai Alashe, Magnus Eriksson, Danny Hoesen, Nick Lima, Jimmy Ockford, Francois Affolter, Kevin Partida, Shea Salinas, Harold Cummings, and Andrew Tarbell. Things will probably shift around, and how San Jose builds off of this nucleus of talent will be the key to its success. Wondolowski should still have a few good years left as he seeks to become the all-time leading MLS scorer. Just how far will he go?

Overall Team Rating: 7.1

SEATTLE SOUNDERS FC

Twitter: @SoundersFC
First season: 2009
MLS Cup: 1
US Open Cup: 4
Supporters' Shield: 1

Known For
Winning the MLS Cup
Sellout games
Insanely loud fans
Insanely dedicated fans
Sigi Schmid
Brian Schmetzer
Clint Dempsey
Brad Evans
Jordan Morris
Nicolas Lodeiro

A BRIEF TEAM HISTORY

Since its first game in 2009, the Sounders have done very well,
earning the MLS Cup, a Supporters' Shield title, and four

US Open Cups. That's a good start for a team that's barely ten years old.

US OPEN CUP

The Sounders have won the US Open Cup four times.

FACTS ABOUT THEIR CITY

Seattle—which has a population of around 3.7 million people in the greater metro area—is the land of lattes (and a little place called Starbucks), Amazon, Microsoft, the Seahawks, and a music scene that was made popular in the early 90s by bands like Pearl Jam and Nirvana.

There are plenty of local beers available in Seattle, including Holy Mountain Brewing Company, Optimism Brewing Company, Flying Lion Brewing, Belltown Brewing, and Jellyfish Brewing Company, to name a few. Restaurants are ubiquitous in Seattle and a few that soccer fans might stumble across are Altura, Sushi Kashiba, Quality Athletics, and Matt's in the Market.

Seattle soccer fans are abundant. Supporters' groups for the Sounders include Emerald City Supporters, Gorilla FC, North End Faithful, and Eastside Supporters.

WHERE THE TEAM IS TODAY: TACTICS AND STRATEGIES

Defensively, the Sounders are a team that can stay in games, likely using a 4-4-2 or 4-2-3-1 formation. Chad Marshall adds experience and leadership in the back; he's played a ton of games in his career with Columbus Crew and Seattle and, if he stays around, he should guide the team in a steady direction.

With Lodeiro, Bruin, and Ruidiaz, offensively, the Sounders have depth, and with some creative inspiration, it's a group aspiring to get back to being a team that gets goals in bunches. This will come from a conscious effort to play with team cohesion, continuity, and a touch of flair.

BRIAN SCHMETZER: A BRIEF COACHING PORTRAIT

With Brian Schmetzer, you get a coach that wants smart soccer played. He doesn't think that crossing multiple balls in from the wings is the best approach to scoring. He was speaking of a 0-0 draw with Columbus Crew from a game in 2018, during which his team had a man advantage (due to one of the Crew players getting ejected). In response to his team being booed, Schmetzer said, "The fact that we had to resort to pumping balls into the box from wide channels is not indicative of the play that we're capable of."[36]

This is indicative of how he views the game overall. Schmetzer—who is originally from Seattle—spent a lot of time playing professional indoor soccer, which may explain his desire to avoid randomly crossing the ball into the box. Indoor stresses quite the opposite, encompassing individual skill and passing in tight areas, which leads to skillful interplay between teammates—an aspect of the game many American fans fell in love with back in the 1980s. This background from Schmetzer's playing experience is a great attribute to have as coach.

Don't be surprised to see a 4-4-2 or perhaps a 4-2-3-1 formation as his team looks to regain a creative touch this season.

KEY PLAYERS AND THEIR CHARACTERISTICS

Clint Dempsey, Nicolas Lodeiro, and Jordan Morris

Clint Dempsey, who recently retired, obviously deserves an honorable mention here. Arguably the best player in American soccer history, Dempsey landed in Seattle after highly productive seasons in England, with Fulham and Tottenham, and he did very well with the Sounders, even toward the end. Dempsey—a Texas native now in his mid-30s—may consider coming out of retirement but that is yet to be seen. Dempsey was a player that always seemed to make the right pass, even if it was a simple go nowhere ball (a pass that eventually leads to something interesting), and he had an uncanny sense of how to score goals. He was a great presence for the Sounders and American soccer in general.

Nicolas Lodeiro—the Uruguayan native with multiple years of experience on his national team—has basically been handed the keys to the Sounders. With his leadership in the midfield, everything seems to rotate around his touch on the ball. A lot of the burden of winning or losing rests on his shoulders. Keep an eye on him in the midfield as the Sounders push forward throughout the season, striving for the MLS Cup.

Jordan Morris—a product of Stanford University—is a young forward coming off a knee injury and hoping to get back into his scoring ways. At times, he's a forward that plays like Rudi Voller, probing defenses with dribbling that allows him to create space to set up a shot or pass.

KEY PLAYER STATS

(Total career goals with this club)

	Games Played	Goals	Scoring Percentage
Clint Dempsey	115	47	40%
Nicolas Lodeiro	73	19	26%
Jordan Morris	57	15	26%

WHAT TO WATCH FOR ON TV: HOW BRADLEY, IBRAHIMOVIC, NAGBE, AND OTHERS PLAY

MLS is bursting with excitement and the Seattle Sounders, along with its fan base and practically everyone involved with the team, should receive many thanks from anyone that appreciates soccer.

There was a window of time—in the post-NASL and pre-1994 years—when it seemed like soccer was done in the United States. So when you see MLS succeeding beyond anyone's wildest imagination, it's in large part due to franchises like that of Seattle. The amazing spectacle of Seattle Sounders home games is exactly what proponents of American soccer envisaged when they were daring enough to galvanize MLS into action in 1996. Their fans are one of kind, and each game comes to life with an outpouring of emotion, team pride, flags, and chants, with a thunderous roar when goals are scored.

Based on past success, and the talent pool that exists within the structure of the club, there might be a fear by some that the 2018 season represented a sort of involuntary abdication from the limelight, but Seattle is one of those teams that will be a presence in the league, with a great fan base, a rich history, and so much potential yet to come. Will it take the Sounders 72 years to win the MLS Cup again? Probably not, but they're in a tough conference, and as the league becomes increasingly competitive it will be a challenge to remain on top of things. As new seasons begin, it is likely that the Seattle team will continue to find a place for itself with smart trades and placing players on the field that will produce.

Currently, as the team finds a balance between possession for possession's sake, and possession with a purpose, it's a group that is fighting to get back to the championship game, to hoist the MLS Cup again. Prior to this season, Dempsey provided a crucial element to Seattle's flow in possession, which positively affected success throughout the duration of a long season. Now, with Dempsey's retirement, that void has to be filled. Ruidiaz is a talented feature up front, with the ability to score goals (and to draw defenders away from Lodeiro) with runs around the box; he's a handful. Also, keep an eye out for contributions from Marshall, Shipp, Cristian (and potentially Alex) Roldan, along with Bruin. Lodeiro is carrying the team, pushing them forward from the midfield, while his supporting cast has the capability to add some punch up front, particularly when they get Jordan Morris back in the swing of things.

Overall Team Rating: 8.1

SPORTING KANSAS CITY

Twitter: @SportingKC
First season: 1996
MLS Cup: 2
US Open Cup: 4
Supporters' Shield: 1

Known For
Being one of the original 10 MLS teams
Very passionate fans
High-end BBQ
Being rivals with a city that doesn't have an MLS team yet (St. Louis)
Chris Klein
Preki
Matt Besler
Graham Zusi

A BRIEF TEAM HISTORY

Originally, Sporting Kansas City were called the Kansas City Wiz, or the Kansas City Wizards. From its place in the Midwest,

Kansas City has been a successful team over the years, capturing two MLS Cups, along with lesser trophies.

US OPEN CUP

Sporting KC has won the US Open Cup four times.

FACTS ABOUT THEIR CITY

Sporting KC play in Children's Mercy Park stadium, which is in Kansas City, Kansas, and it holds a little over 18,000 for soccer games.

Kansas City is known for BBQ and plenty of beer. It's also known for straddling two states, Kansas and Missouri. In the metro area of Kansas City, Missouri, there is a population of just over 2 million people, while Kansas City, Kansas, has a population of around 150,000 people. There are many local beers available for fans, including a variety from Border Brewing Company, Double Shift Brewing Company, and Boulevard Brewing Company.

You're always going to get fun, interesting, family-friendly restaurants around the greater Kansas City area, including Lidia's Kansas City, Michael Smith Restaurant, and Seasons 52, all located in Kansas City, Missouri. In Kansas City, Kansas, you might stumble across Slap's BBQ, among other places.

While home games are in session, Sporting KC supporters' groups The Cauldron and South Stand SC will be nearby.

WHERE THE TEAM IS TODAY: TACTICS AND STRATEGIES

Offensively, Sporting Kansas City relies on smart passing, with combinations, often across the field, edging forward, waiting for a knockout punch. With that said, it's a patient team, one that plays the game well, and, over the long haul, its effective approach in the possession game has taken this club a long way.

Defensively, with the leadership of Matt Besler, it's a team that is organized and that applies pressure to its opponents in an effort to limit their space, which creates counters the other way.

Under the guidance of coach Peter Vermes, Sporting KC will likely field a 4-3-3 formation.

PETER VERMES: A BRIEF COACHING PORTRAIT

Peter Vermes—a native of New Jersey—was a longtime member of the USMNT. He played professionally for many teams, including the Colorado Rapids and Kansas City Wizards.

As a coach of Sporting Kansas City, his team plays with a certain flow; he seems to be doing something right. This starts with the recruitment of players that he feels will act out his vision, and then the implementation of his game plan into the actions the players take on the field. His teams have a good sense of creating combinations through passing, which is accentuated by proper spacing throughout the pitch and a timely rhythm. The players are confident; they're not afraid to dribble, and they combine dribbling with passing combinations nicely. In the larger scheme of things, they look more like a European club than a traditional American one. To put it succinctly, there's a good flow. Win or lose, Vermes deserves credit for this.

It wouldn't be surprising to see a 4-3-3 formation as Sporting Kansas City moves forward this season, on its way to achieving high-quality soccer.

KEY PLAYERS AND THEIR CHARACTERISTICS

Graham Zusi and Matt Besler

Graham Zusi is a longtime member of the USMNT, usually found at outside midfield. He's a steady presence, with good technique and field vision. As a veteran, he adds his wealth of national team experience to Sporting KC's locker room. He's an important member of the team and things seem to work around him in the attack.

Matt Besler, like Zusi, is an experienced player with the USMNT. He's been called on plenty of times to represent his country, and with Sporting Kansas City, he brings a ton of international experience to every practice and game. As a defender, Besler has good skill and technique—better than most—and he uses this ability to guide Sporting KC forward in the possession game.

KEY PLAYER STATS

(Total career goals with this club)

	Games Played	Goals	Scoring Percentage
Graham Zusi	252	28	11%
Matt Besler	257	3	1%

WHAT TO WATCH FOR ON TV: HOW BRADLEY, IBRAHIMOVIC, NAGBE, AND OTHERS PLAY

Sporting Kansas City is very well-coached by Peter Vermes, a former USMNT standout. From the mind of Vermes, there's a flow Sporting KC has to its possession, which yields good results, along with calm pleasant periods (which, for aficionados, is nice to watch), accompanied by intermittent bursts of excitement.

Brad Evans—an experienced player from Seattle Sounders FC—arrived at Sporting Kansas City last season; should he stay with the team, he'll add value in the midfield and defense.

Tim Melia—Sporting KC's goalkeeper—is a base of security for the team. He was the winner of the 2017 MLS Goalkeeper of the Year Award.

Roger Espinoza, Daniel Salloi, Yohan Croizet, and Khiry Shelton were among some of the names available to Sporting Kansas City in 2018; it was a strong year, with a lot to build on. Look for them, along with some potential changes, in the 2019 season.

Besler—who is originally from Kansas—creates a strong presence both defensively, with organizational awareness, and offensively, with his ability to distribute the ball in possession. Zusi adds another level of calm to the distribution end of things, which allows the supporting cast room to implement steady waves of attacking soccer.

Overall Team Rating: 9.3

VANCOUVER WHITECAPS FC

Twitter: @WhitecapsFC
First season: 2011
MLS Cup: 0
US Open Cup: 0
Supporters' Shield: 0

Known For
Passionate fans
Appreciation of soccer
Amazing city
Jay DeMerit

A BRIEF TEAM HISTORY

The Whitecaps may not have titles yet, but it's a team that has risen again, taking on the honor of paving a new path for soccer in Vancouver. Before this incarnation of the Whitecaps, there were other teams with the same name, though this time around it's with a league that is driven to succeed.

US OPEN CUP

To date, this Canadian soccer team has zero titles within the US Open Cup, but, back in 2015, the Whitecaps won the Canadian Championship.

FACTS ABOUT THEIR CITY

Vancouver has a population of around 2.4 million people in the greater metro area.

The team's stadium is called BC Place, which was built in the early 1980s and holds around 22,000 people.

If you happen to be in Vancouver, and you feel like beer, you might want to try Strange Fellows Brewing Company and Powell Brewery. Vancouver Whitecaps FC supporters' groups sure to be enjoying beer include Southsiders, Curva Collective, and Rain City Brigade.

WHERE THE TEAM IS TODAY: TACTICS AND STRATEGIES

Offensively, this is a team with some skill and an ability to combine passes around the top of the box, along with experienced players, such as Kendall Waston with the Costa Rican national team.

Defensively, likely in the formation of a 4-4-2, the Whitecaps have been lucky to attain the past services of Waston and Felipe. Should they remain with the squad, prospects for the Whitecaps are good, as it's a team that has interesting components in place, seeking its first MLS Cup.

MARC DOS SANTOS: A BRIEF COACHING PORTRAIT

Craig Dalrymple took on the coaching position of Vancouver in 2018, during a tough season in which the Whitecaps were not attaining the best results they could have. It was unclear how permanent Dalrymple's appointment to head coach would be. In fact, prior to 2019, he was replaced by Marc Dos Santos. Dos Santos, who was born in Canada, has a big job ahead, one that involves guiding an average team to a better place, which, given the fact that Vancouver has zero championships in MLS, will be a challenge to say the least. Whether he remains or someone else takes the job, the Whitecaps have a window of opportunity to rebuild on its quest to reach the top of the standings.

KEY PLAYERS AND THEIR CHARACTERISTICS

Kendall Waston, Felipe, and Yordy Reyna

Kendall Waston is a central defender from Costa Rica with time spent on his very talented national team. He has over 100 games played with Vancouver. As the team moves forward, seeking its first MLS Cup, he is definitely an experienced player to keep around.

Felipe adds a Brazilian touch to the midfield. The South American has plenty of experience from his previous time with Montreal Impact and New York Red Bulls.

Yordy Reyna—who has a few caps with the Peruvian national team—is a skillful, crafty forward; keep an eye out for him to potentially make give-and-goes around the box as he increases his scoring tally.

KEY PLAYER STATS

(Total career goals with this club)

	Games Played	Goals	Scoring Percentage
Kendall Waston	115	14	12%
Felipe	29	1	3%
Yordy Reyna	44	12	27%

WHAT TO WATCH FOR ON TV: HOW BRADLEY, IBRAHIMOVIC, NAGBE, AND OTHERS PLAY

Anthony Blondell, Felipe, Nicolas Mezquida, Ali Ghazal, Marcel de Jong, Yordy Reyna, Kei Kamara, and Erik Hurtado were available for the Whitecaps in 2018. Whether they remain with the team throughout the 2019 season is another story; losing sides and middle-of-the-road teams tend to roll the dice here and there so don't be surprised to see a new look on the roster as the year moves on. Last year, Vancouver was often balancing somewhere in the middle.

It's a middle-of-the-road team with so much potential to be a lower top-end team. How can they achieve this? Recruit more skillful players (like Shea, who was a great signing), and improve the on-field team chemistry. Sounds easy enough, and it's very possible for the Whitecaps. Vancouver is a great city, with great people, great fans, a strong soccer following, and a beautiful stadium. Things are only looking up. With many capable pieces on the chessboard, it's a team that's on the rise, hungry for a title and looking to shake things up.

Overall Team Rating: 7.1

A LOOK FORWARD TO THE 2019 MLS SEASON

BUDGETS 2019

The matter of budgets and player salaries has been discussed for years. The 2019 MLS season has been affected by previous negotiations that are only now coming to fruition. In 2015, according to the *Chicago Tribune,* MLS players "ratified their five-year collective bargaining agreement that runs through the 2019 season. The MLS Players Union said Thursday that 91 percent of its members voted in favor of the deal announced March 5, a day before the season opener. MLS spokesman Dan Courtemanche said owners also have approved the agreement. The minimum salary for the first 24 players on each roster rises from $48,500 to $60,000 this season, $62,500 in 2016, $65,000 in 2017, $67,500 in 2018, and $70,250 in 2019. The minimum for remaining players, who must be 24 or younger, increases from $36,500 last season to $50,000 this year, $51,500 in 2016, $53,000 in 2017, $54,500 in 2018, and $56,250 in 2019. Players earning the lower minimum receive bonuses of $500 per league game appearance and an additional $750 per league start. The union estimates the average salary of players on the senior roster will rise by about $60,000 during the agreement and approach $200,000 by 2019."[37]

2019 CONCACAF CHAMPIONS LEAGUE

Sixteen teams competed for the title of CONCACAF champion, a title that is gaining more prestige as time marches on. The United States got four berths, Canada got one. The tournament will take place from February to April 2019. Sporting Kansas City and Toronto FC have strong teams going in. Both teams are likely contenders for the title in this elite tournament of champions for teams from North America, Central America, and the Caribbean. (This book should be in print before the tournament has finished. For results, visit MLS online, US Soccer online, or Wikipedia.)

2019 US OPEN CUP

The 2019 US Open Cup will be as competitive as ever. Top teams going into the tournament will be Atlanta United FC, New York City Red Bulls, New York City FC, Sporting Kansas City, FC Dallas, and Los Angeles FC.

Amateur teams play a large role in the tournament, as they dream of getting through to the later rounds. According to US Soccer, "seventy-six amateur teams begin their dream of qualifying for the 2019 Lamar Hunt US Open Cup this weekend, just days before the 2018 edition of the oldest ongoing national soccer competition in the United States wraps up. On September 22-23, 76 of the 94 local amateur sides that entered Open Division Local Qualifying for the 2019 tournament will contest the first qualifying round. Divided into six geographical groupings, the Southeast, Central, and Mountain Regions will see a combined 28 teams meet in the first single-game, knockout qualifying round. An additional 10 teams from these three regions received first round byes and will commence qualifying in the second round on October 20-21 along with the 14 winners from the first weekend."[38]

The tournament really gets going around mid-summer 2019. Look forward to results then. (This book should be published prior to the ongoing tournament being in full swing. For results, visit MLS online, US Soccer online, or Wikipedia.)

RECORDS AND STATISTICS

MLS SINGLE-SEASON SCORING RECORD

1. Josef Martinez (2018)	31	
2. Roy Lassiter (1996)	27	
2. Chris Wondolowski (2012)	27	
2. Bradley Wright-Phillips (2014)	27	

It happened! Josef Martinez—the dazzling forward from Atlanta United FC—broke the single-season scoring record. Originally, the record was held by Roy Lassiter, who scored 27 goals in 1996 while playing for Tampa Bay Mutiny. Since that time, the record was tied by Chris Wondolowski in 2012, playing for San Jose Earthquakes, and Bradley Wright-Phillips in 2014, playing for New York Red Bulls.

On August 24, 2018, Martinez took the helm with his 28th goal of the season. He eventually shattered the record with a total of 31 goals for the 2018 MLS season.

In 2018, Bradley Wright-Phillips reached 100 goals in the fastest amount of time (within 159 games)—an MLS record.

MLS CUP CHAMPIONS

Since the inception of MLS in 1996, a few teams have earned a place in history. To be champions of a league that has such great promise and that will likely be around for a long time is a great honor.

MLS Cup Champions List
1996
D.C. United

1997
D.C. United

1998
Chicago Fire

1999
D.C. United

2000
Kansas City Wizards

2001
San Jose Earthquakes

2002
LA Galaxy

2003
San Jose Earthquakes

2004
D.C. United

2005
LA Galaxy

2006
Houston Dynamo

2007
Houston Dynamo

2008
Columbus Crew

2009
Real Salt Lake

2010
Colorado Rapids

2011
LA Galaxy

2012
LA Galaxy

2013
Sporting Kansas City

2014
LA Galaxy

2015
Portland Timbers

2016
Seattle Sounders

2017
Toronto FC

2018
Atlanta United FC

All-Time MLS Scoring Leaders
1. Landon Donovan 145

2. Chris Wondolowski* 144

3. Jeff Cunningham 134

4. Jaime Moreno 133

5. Ante Rasov 114

6. Jason Kreis 108

7. Dwayne De Rosario 104

8. Taylor Twellman 101

---

*   Still playing.

9. Kei Kamara† 100

10. Edson Buddle 100

All-Time MLS Assist Leaders
1. Landon Donovan 136

2. Steve Ralston 135

3. Brad Davis 123

4. Carlos Valderrama 114

5. Preki 112

MLS Most Valuable Player Award (AKA The Landon Donovan MVP Award)
1996
Carlos Valderrama (Tampa Bay Mutiny)

1997
Preki (Kansas City Wizards)

1998
Marco Etcheverry (D.C. United)

1999
Jason Kreis (Dallas Burn)

---

†   Still playing.

2000
Tony Meola (Kansas City Wizards)

2001
Alex Pineda Chacon (Miami Fusion)

2002
Carlos Ruiz (LA Galaxy)

2003
Preki (Kansas City Wizards)

2004
Amado Guevara (New York/New Jersey MetroStars)

2005
Taylor Twellman (New England Revolution)

2006
Christian Gomez (D.C. United)

2007
Luciano Emilio (D.C. United)

2008
Guillermo Barros Schelotto (Columbus Crew)

2009
Landon Donovan (LA Galaxy)

2010
David Ferreira (FC Dallas)

2011
Dwayne De Rosario (D.C. United)

2012
Chris Wondolowski (San Jose Earthquakes)

2013
Mike Magee (Chicago Fire)

2014
Robbie Keane (LA Galaxy)

2015
Sebastian Giovinco (Toronto FC)

2016
David Villa (New York City FC)

2017
Diego Valeri (Portland Timbers)

2018
Josef Martinez (Atlanta United FC)

MLS Goalkeeper of the Year Award
1996
Mark Dodd (Dallas Burn)

1997
Brad Friedel (Columbus Crew)

1998
Zach Thornton (Chicago Fire)

1999
Kevin Hartman (LA Galaxy)

2000
Tony Meola (Kansas City Wizards)

2001
Tim Howard (New York/New Jersey MetroStars)

2002
Joe Cannon (San Jose Earthquakes)

2003
Pat Onstad (San Jose Earthquakes)

2004
Joe Cannon (Colorado Rapids)

2005
Pat Onstad (San Jose Earthquakes)

2006
Troy Perkins (D.C. United)

2007
Brad Guzan (Chivas USA)

2008
Jon Busch (Chicago Fire)

2009
Zach Thornton (Chivas USA)

2010
Donovan Ricketts (LA Galaxy)

2011
Kasey Keller (Seattle Sounders FC)

2012
Jimmy Nielsen (Sporting Kansas City)

2013
Donovan Ricketts (Portland Timbers)

2014
Bill Hamid (D.C. United)

2015
Luis Robles (New York Red Bulls)

2016
Andre Blake (Philadelphia Union)

2017
Tim Melia (Sporting Kansas City)

2018
Zack Steffen (Columbus Crew)

The Stay-or-Leave Awards for 2018

(These are the fun awards not necessarily given out by league administrators.)

Most interesting mascot: Kingston (Orlando City SC)

Best MLS home-game fans: Seattle and Portland

Best team uniforms: Sporting Kansas City

Best MLS team that doesn't exist yet: St. Louis

Best MLS coach: Gerardo Martino (Atlanta United FC)

Best goal of the year: A great tackle and assist from Rooney that resulted in a game-winning header from Acosta

Best MLS scorer: Josef Martinez

Best MLS goalkeeper: Brad Guzan

Best MLS midfielder: Miguel Almiron

Best MLS forward: Josef Martinez

The Top 10 Offensive Players of the 2018 MLS Season

1. Josef Martinez (Atlanta United FC)

2. Sebastian Giovinco (Toronto FC)

3. Zlatan Ibrahimovic (LA Galaxy)

4. Miguel Almiron (Atlanta United FC)

5. Carlos Vela (Los Angeles FC)

6. Wayne Rooney (D.C. United)

7. David Villa (New York City FC)

8. Bradley Wright-Phillips (New York Red Bulls)

9. Lee Nguyen (Los Angeles FC)

10. Diego Valeri (Portland Timbers)

TRIVIA

Questions

1. Against what team did Josef Martinez score his record-breaking 28th goal?

2. Who was coach of LAFC during the 2018 season?

3. Which team did Dom Dwyer play for in 2018?

4. Brek Shea suited up for Vancouver in 2018. What state is he originally from?

5. Fans from a particular MLS team have been known to take over a section of their own stadium. Which team do they support?

6. Which team had the most players in the 2018 MLS All-Star Game?

7. Which MLS team did Tyler Adams play for in 2018?

8. Which MLS team did Wayne Rooney play for in 2018?

9. What country is Miguel Almiron from?

10. As of 2018, who are the three players tied for second place with 27 goals scored in a season?

Answers

1. Orlando City SC

2. Bob Bradley

3. Orlando City SC

4. Texas

5. Chicago Fire

6. Atlanta United FC

7. New York City Red Bulls

8. D.C. United

9. Paraguay

10. Roy Lassiter, Chris Wondolowski, and Bradley Wright-Phillips

FUNNY AND STRANGE MLS STORIES AND ANECDOTES

After years of success in MLS, Columbus Crew found itself in the middle of a lawsuit to stay in Columbus; there were even efforts to relocate to Austin, Texas. All this drama and talk of potential relocation came right when Cincinnati—a perfect in-state rival for Columbus—was about to enter the league.

St. Louis, the cradle of soccer in the United States, still does not have an MLS team.

Zlatan Ibrahimovic decided not to play in the 2018 MLS All-Star Game against Juventus.

Orlando City SC was the recipient of one of the greatest goals in MLS history, whereby Wayne Rooney backtracked to make a solo tackle of the ball, then played a long cross-field ball to Acosta's head for a game-winning goal.

But Orlando wasn't finished, later allowing Josef Martinez to score his 28th goal of the season, an MLS record.

In 2018, Chicago Fire fans briefly took over a section of their own stadium.

Bradley Wright-Phillips had a big year in 2018 with the Red Bulls. The man with a knack for scoring made MLS history after reaching 100 goals in the fastest amount of time (within 159 games).

D.C. United, a team that lingered in the lower end of the Eastern Conference standings for much of 2018, made a surprise run at the end of the season and eventually placed fourth.

MLS FANTASY LEAGUE 2019 GUIDE

POWER PLAYERS

Get the top players fast to help guide your fantasy team! The ranking is out of 10 (10 being the highest). Players are ranked on their individual skillsets, past performances, international experience (if applicable), accomplishments, age, and their team's success. For instance, Orlando City players did not get high rankings, largely based on their team's bad season in 2018, which would indicate similar things to come in 2019.

Players not mentioned are not necessarily undesirable; there might be more information about a player you are interested in which would be located in the team's section within this book.

Eastern Conference

Josef Martinez	10
Darlington Nagbe	10
Ezequiel Barco	9.5
Hector Villalba	9.3
Julian Gressel	9.5
Jeff Larentowicz	9
Michael Parkhurst	9.6
Bastian Schweinsteiger	9

Dax McCarty	8.5
Gyasi Zardes	8
Wil Trapp	8.4
Ricardo Clark	7.8
Paul Arriola	8.8
Wayne Rooney	9.9
Luciano Acosta	8.9
Ignacio Piatti	9.7
Samuel Piette	7.8
Scott Caldwell	7
Teal Bunbury	7
Maximiliano Moralez	8
David Villa	9.9
Thomas McNamara	7
Bradley Wright-Phillips	9.8
Tyler Adams	8
Kaku	8
Kemar Lawrence	8.9
Tim Parker	7
Dom Dwyer	6.9
Will Johnson	7
Sacha Kljestan	6.8
Fafa Picault	7
Alejandro Bedoya	7
Sebastian Giovinco	9.8
Michael Bradley	9
Marky Delgado	7.5
Forrest Lasso	7
Corben Bone	7
Fanendo Adi	7

Goalies:

Brad Guzan	9.9
Zack Steffen	9.8
Andre Blake	9

Western Conference

Giles Barnes	7
Jack Price	7
Johan Blomberg	7
Michael Barrios	8.8
Paxton Pomykal	7
Reggie Cannon	8
DaMarcus Beasley	7.1
Arturo Alvarez	8
Tomas Martinez	8
Zlatan Ibrahimovic	9.9
Giovani dos Santos	9
Sebastian Lletget	7.5
Ashley Cole	9
Emmanuel Boateng	9
Perry Kitchen	8
Chris Pontius	8
Carlos Vela	9.8
Diego Rossi	8.5
Benny Feilhaber	8.3
Lee Nguyen	9.5
Miguel Ibarra	7.8
Ibson	8
Diego Valeri	9.6
Sebastian Blanco	9

Kyle Beckerman	7.8-8.1
Joao Plata	7
Chris Wondolowski	9.5
Danny Hoesen	8
Nicolas Lodeiro	9.4
Jordan Morris	8
Graham Zusi	9
Matt Besler	9
Break Shea	9.1
Kendall Waston	7
Felipe	8
Yordy Reyna	7-8

Goalies:

Tim Howard	9
Tyler Miller	9
Nick Rimando	9

MLS FANTASY LEAGUE 2019
TEAM RANKING

(Teams in bold qualified for the Audi 2018 MLS Cup Playoffs)

Eastern Conference
1 Atlanta United FC
2 New York Red Bulls
3 New York City FC
4 D.C. United
5 Columbus Crew
6 Philadelphia Union

7 Montreal Impact
8 New England Revolution
9 Toronto FC
10 Chicago Fire
11 Orlando City SC

Western Conference
1 Sporting Kansas City
2 Seattle Sounders FC
3 Los Angeles FC
4 FC Dallas
5 Portland Timbers
6 Real Salt Lake
7 LA Galaxy
8 Vancouver Whitecaps FC
9 Houston Dynamo
10 Minnesota United FC
11 Colorado Rapids
12 San Jose Earthquakes

AUTHOR'S NOTE

Useful information regarding players, teams, and other matters of interest was gathered from *The New York Times*, *The Washington Post*, *Los Angeles Times*, *USA Today*, *The Seattle Times*, and many others. A special thanks to those publications—and all sources listed within—for their work.

All information within this book is up to date. Every piece of information that was researched was placed in the book as close to publication as possible. Furthermore, critical information (such as a goal count for an individual player) was gathered up to the last minute before this book was published.

Teams change frequently; for example, players are often traded, coaches move around, and so on. The players listed within this book are projected players for the 2019 MLS season, and they are as current as possible, though it's common knowledge that rosters fluctuate frequently. All populations are approximate and were acquired from Wikipedia in 2018.

Each player's goals and scoring percentage are not based on a single season. Rather, these statistics are based on their overall contribution, throughout their entire duration with the team in question. The goal count was acquired from Wikipedia. This statistic will likely change over the course of time. (Keep in mind that some players might have been injured and did not play all games, or missed some games because of a transfer.) The scoring percentages were not rounded off.

The overall team rating is based on teams within MLS. It is not comparing MLS teams to Manchester United, Bayern Munich, or any other professional teams from around the world. The rating is on a scale of 1-10, with 10 being the highest.

A special thanks to all the representatives of restaurants and bars that took part in interviews for this book. Further thanks to MLS team representatives that answered questions and provided valuable information. Thanks also to US Soccer for answering questions.

Major League Soccer is very new. Yet, as it tries to catch up with premiere leagues around the world, leagues with an advantageous head start, MLS is destined to rival such company. The United States is the athletic standard around the world, with the exception of men's soccer, America's last athletic frontier. MLS represents a cornerstone for the US to begin its dominance in international soccer. Many people are investing practically every ounce of American athletic know-how into MLS, with finances, facilities, youth academies, marketing, player recruitment, training techniques, and the expansion of a league ready for greatness. Major League Soccer is, without a doubt, destined to become the world's next super league.

APPENDIX

AMERICANS AGAINST SOCCER

There have been many reasons why mainstream Americans don't like soccer. For years, it has been viewed as a sport that less talented athletes play. Americans view baseball, football, and basketball as the top athletic sports. Traditionally, they tend to think that since the best athletes play football and basketball, soccer gets the leftovers. It's also sometimes seen as a girly European sport that men with accents play. It's just not manly enough for many Americans.

Many Americans are convinced soccer is too boring to watch. These are the same Americans that spend the happiest moments of their lives sitting in front of a TV watching golf and NASCAR. Slowly, over time, like continental drift, a large number of mainstream Americans have come around to appreciating soccer.

A LOOK BACK AT THE 2018 USMNT SEASON

As many of the USMNT players circulate throughout MLS, it is reasonable to include a brief look at the USMNT during 2018.

In 2018, even without the US in the World Cup, there was a lot going on with the USMNT. The last time the USMNT did not make a World Cup was 1986. Since 1990, the USMNT has participated in every tournament, and getting there is a big deal. Prior to 1990, the USMNT had not qualified for the World Cup since 1950! (Reaching the World Cup of 1990 was the result of the shot heard round the world as Paul Caligiuri delivered the famous goal—a miraculous volley from distance—that defeated Trinidad and Tobago on the road in a must-win game.) Obviously, not qualifying for World Cup 2018 was big news.

In July 2018, during the world's biggest athletic tournament in Russia, in a piece from *The Wall Street Journal*, Rachel Bachman put things in perspective for American soccer, writing that "the World Cup is moving to the semifinal round. But for a US team that failed to qualify for the first time since 1986, the tournament is just another torturous reminder that the world's richest nation, and one of the most populous, didn't make it."[39]

The topic of head coach for the USMNT was very popular in 2017 and 2018. Following the USMNT's loss to Trinidad and Tobago, Bruce Arena—who had been called in to replace Jurgen Klinsmann at the last minute—stepped down from coaching the team. This was Arena's second term as head coach, having previously led the team in the 2002 and 2006 World Cup.

American soccer fans may have been disappointed, but other teams had a similar fate. As it turned out, it wasn't the best year for top teams around the world. Italy, Holland, and Chile did not qualify for World Cup 2018 either. Italy is one of the best teams in world-soccer history, with four World Cup titles, and Holland is a former European Cup champion, known as one of the best teams to never win the World Cup, while Chile had won the 2015 and 2016 Copa America tournaments. Sometimes, even the best teams need to hit the reset button.

US Soccer—under the leadership of President Sunil Gulati in 2017—replaced Arena with Dave Sarachan, an experienced player and coach, who had previously attended Cornell University and who also happened to be a long-time friend and associate of Arena's. Initially, Sarachan was thought to be an interim coach. This appointment was done in haste as the USMNT had a friendly lined up with Portugal, the 2016 European champions. (The game ended up being a 1-1 tie.) It was generally assumed that a new head coach (i.e., someone other than Sarachan) would be around the corner. According to *The New York Times*, "the search for Arena's long-term replacement will begin in earnest after the Portugal game, but it remains unclear how long the process will take."[40] Following that Portugal game, Sarachan remained as the coach throughout 2018. Names for a possible replacement were tossed around, such as Tab Ramos and Gregg Berhalter.

During 2018, Earnie Stewart—the former USMNT midfielder—was hired as general manager of the USMNT, which, in some people's eyes, was a vague position. Despite this move, Sarachan remained, and speculation continued to linger. Amidst the turmoil of the USMNT and the direction it was trying to take while finding a permanent replacement for head coach, the common view on the street was that of uncertainty. After all, during this time, Clint Dempsey, who was tied with Landon Donovan as the all-time USMNT scorer with 57, was close to finishing his days with the national team, and that was pivotal, because for years he and Donovan had led the team like no other duo before, bringing much success. Dempsey was arguably the best player the US had ever fielded, so to have him running out his last days was definitely a changing of the guard for the program; with that came the realization that new players were needed to fill the void left behind from Dempsey and Donovan. Christian Pulisic and Darlington Nagbe were thought to be the new leaders of the team, along with up-and-coming talents Timothy Weah and Josh Sargent.

Then it became official. After much speculation, US Soccer announced in December of 2018 that Gregg Berhalter was the new head coach of the USMNT. Born in 1973, Berhalter, a New Jersey native, ended up playing with the USMNT for many years, with over 40 games to his credit. What's more, he acquired valuable experience as a professional defender in Holland, along with other places, eventually landing with the LA Galaxy. Prior to accepting the USMNT job, he was coach of Columbus Crew.

While a coaching and talent transition may be exciting, it also carries much trepidation considering the failure to qualify for World Cup 2018, and the unpredictable path ahead as the program gears up for a run at Qatar 2022.

USMNT GAMES OF 2018

The following are games played by the USMNT during 2018, listed in chronological order.

United States vs Bosnia and Herzegovina
1-28-18
Friendly
0-0
Played in Carson, California

United States vs Bolivia
5-28-18
Friendly
3-0
Walker Zimmerman
Josh Sargent
Tim Weah
Played in Chester, Pennsylvania
Talen Energy Stadium

United States vs Ireland
6-2-18
Friendly
1-2
Bobby Wood
Played in Dublin, Ireland
Aviva Stadium

United States vs France
6-9-18
Friendly
1-1
Green
Played in France

United States vs Brazil
9-7-18
Friendly
0-2
Played in East Rutherford, New Jersey

United States vs Mexico
9-11-18
Friendly
1-0
Tyler Adams
Played in Nashville, Tennessee

In October and November of 2018, the USMNT had further friendly matches with Colombia, Peru, England, and Italy. These were great match-ups for the US men; each game featured a worthy opponent, particularly at the end with England and Italy. Somewhat similar to England and Italy, the US was a program in a building process, searching for success and hungry to reach the top of the charts. (While the US doesn't have the glorious international résumé that England and Italy have, all three programs have been in the process of reevaluating things.) More friendlies with quality opponents like these will only help the USMNT on its quest to winning the World Cup.

United States vs Colombia
10-11-18
Friendly
2-4
Kellyn Acosta
Bobby Wood
Played in Tampa, Florida
Raymond James Stadium

United States vs Peru

10-16-18

Friendly

1-1

Josh Sargent

Played in East Hartford, Connecticut

Rentschler Field

United States vs England

11-15-18

Friendly

0-3

Played in London, England

Wembley Stadium

United States vs Italy

11-20-18

Friendly

0-1

Played in Belgium

A LOOK AHEAD TO THE 2019 USMNT SEASON

The USMNT is looking forward to a strong showing in 2019, with new players on the radar, including Timothy Weah, the son of George Weah,* and Josh Sargent,† a product of Scott Gallagher in St. Louis, Missouri.

A great training ground for the development of the USMNT has been Major League Soccer and the opportunity it affords players to compete at a high level. The academy programs of MLS teams are also contributing to this player development, getting youth talent ready for MLS, which also prepares them for the national team, should they be called upon to join it.

The road to 2019 and beyond started with a shake-up in leadership within US Soccer (also known as the United States Soccer Federation, USSF). Carlos Cordeiro became president on February 10, 2018. He replaced Sunil Gulati, who had been president from March 11, 2006, until February 10, 2018.

A new coach was in order as well. Dave Sarachan's extended run as interim head coach saw many new players enter the mix. Sarachan was doing his best to guide the team forward, as rebuilding continued. Talk regarding a new coach throughout 2018 turned into reality as Gregg Berhalter stepped into the job.

---

* George Weah played for a number of teams, including AC Milan, and he won FIFA World Player of the Year in 1995. On January 22, 2018, he became president of Liberia.

† Neither of Josh Sargent's parents have been president of Liberia.

With Berhalter as coach, the USMNT has a new outlook on life, along with many challenges in the near future. The biggest challenge will be getting into the 2022 World Cup. Berhalter is undoubtedly aware of this. While MLS plays a strong role in nurturing the players, and gearing them up for top-level competition, it should be an interesting run for Berhalter and the players he brings on board.

ENDNOTES

1   Ken Belson, "*As Appetite for Soccer in U.S. Grows, So Does M.L.S.,*" *The New York Times*, published August 8, 2017, accessed August 5, 2018, https://www.nytimes.com/2017/08/08/sports/soccer/mls-expansion-nashville-cincinnati.html

2   *Wikipedia, The Free Encyclopedia*, s.vv. "North American Soccer League (1968-84)," accessed August 5, 2018, https://en.wikipedia.org/wiki/North_American_Soccer_League_(1968%E2%80%9384)

3   R.W. Apple Jr., "*Pele to Play Soccer Here for $7-Million,*" *The New York Times*, published June 4, 1975, accessed August 5, 2018, https://www.nytimes.com/1975/06/04/archives/pele-to-play-soccer-here-for-7million-pele-agrees-to-cosmos-pact.html

4   *Wikipedia, The Free Encyclopedia*, s.vv. "USSF (United States Soccer Federation) also known as U.S. Soccer," accessed May 18, 2018, https://en.wikipedia.org/wiki/United_States_Soccer_Federation

5   Norman Chad, "The problem with the rapid expansion of professional soccer in America," *The Washington Post*, published May 6, 2018, accessed July 23, 2018, https://www.washingtonpost.com/sports/the-problem-with-the-rapid-expansion-of-professional-soccer-

in-america/2018/05/06/f690dfe0-50d2-11e8-84a0-458a1aa9ac0a_story.
html?utm_term=.2a00a8f04d7c

6   *Wikipedia, The Free Encyclopedia*, s.vv. "Designated Player Rule,"
accessed July 21, 2018, https://en.wikipedia.org/wiki/Designated_
Player_Rule

7   Nick Rosano, "2018 MLS All-Star Fan XI presented by Target,"
MLS website, mlssoccer.com, published June 25, 2018, accessed August
3, 2018, https://www.mlssoccer.com/post/2017/06/25/2018-mls-all-star-
fan-xi-presented-by-target

8   MLSsoccer staff, "Audi 2018 MLS Cup Playoffs schedule
revealed, final to be played on Dec. 8," *MLS website, mlssoccer.com*,
published September 5, 2018, accessed September 12, 2018, https://
www.mlssoccer.com/post/2018/09/05/audi-2018-mls-cup-playoffs-
schedule-revealed-final-be-played-dec-8

9   *Wikipedia, The Free Encyclopedia*, s.vv. "U.S. Open Cup soccer,"
accessed July 7, 2018, https://en.wikipedia.org/wiki/U.S._Open_
Cup#cite_note-CCL2008-3

10   Jim Reineking, "English star Wayne Rooney completes move to
D.C. United of Major League Soccer," *USA Today*, published June 27,
2018, updated June 28, 2018, accessed July 28, 2018, https://www.
usatoday.com/story/sports/soccer/2018/06/27/wayne-rooney-move-dc-
united-mls/740798002/

11   Norman Chad, "The problem with the rapid expansion of
professional soccer in America," *The Washington Post*, published May
6, 2018, accessed July 23, 2018, https://www.washingtonpost.com/

sports/the-problem-with-the-rapid-expansion-of-professional-soccer-in-america/2018/05/06/f690dfe0-50d2-11e8-84a0-458a1aa9ac0a_story.html?utm_term=.2a00a8f04d7c

12   Ian Quillen, "Jorge Mas, David Beckham set to unveil details of new Miami stadium plan," *MLS website, mlssoccer.com*, published July 9, 2018, accessed July 9, 2018, https://www.mlssoccer.com/post/2018/07/09/jorge-mas-david-beckham-set-unveil-details-new-miami-stadium-plan

13   Nick Rosano, "Nashville awarded MLS expansion club," *MLS website, mlssoccer.com*, published December 20, 2017, accessed July 30, 2018, https://www.mlssoccer.com/post/2017/12/20/nashville-awarded-mls-expansion-club

14   Justin Owen, "Nashville Taxpayers Subsidize Soccer. What's Next, Curling?" *The Wall Street Journal*, published January 19, 2018, accessed July 30, 2018, https://www.wsj.com/articles/nashville-taxpayers-subsidize-soccer-whats-next-curling-1516403555

15   Daniel Boniface and Joe Nguyen, "MLS player salaries 2018: Highest paid players," *The Denver Post*, published May 10, 2018, updated July 11, 2018, accessed September 19, 2018, https://www.denverpost.com/2018/05/10/mls-player-salaries-2018-highest-paid-players/?productCode=WebAccessSP

16   MLS Communications, "MLS Roster Rules and Regulations 2018," *MLS website, mlssoccer.com*, published March 2, 2018, accessed September 18, 2018, https://www.mlssoccer.com/league/official-rules/mls-roster-rules-and-regulations

17   Andrew Das, "*M.L.S. Preview: Three Stories to Watch*," *The New York Times*, published March 3, 2018, accessed July 22, 2018, https://www.nytimes.com/2018/03/03/sports/soccer/mls-preview-.html

18   AP, "Martinez has MLS-record 6th hat trick in Atlanta United win," *USA Today*, published July 21, 2,018, accessed August 13, 2018, https://www.usatoday.com/story/sports/mls/2018/07/21/martinez-has-mls-record-6th-hat-trick-in-atlanta-united-win/37039423/

19   Juan Pimiento, "Chicago Fire lose their 4th straight as fan protests ramp up," *Los Angeles Times*, published July 21, 2018, accessed July 22, 2018, http://www.latimes.com/ct-90mins-chicago-fire-lose-their-4th-straight-amid-more-fan-protests-20180721-story.html

20   John Kass, "Column: Chicago Fire fans want Tom Ricketts to buy their team, too," *Chicago Tribune*, published May 10, 2018, accessed September 13, 2018, http://www.chicagotribune.com/news/columnists/kass/ct-met-tom-ricketts-soccer-kass-0511-story.html

21   Andrew Erickson, "Crew SC 1, Red Bulls 1 | Crew settles for tie, remains unbeaten in nine games," *The Columbus Dispatch*, published June 9, 2018, updated June 10, 2018, accessed September 12, 2018, http://www.dispatch.com/sports/20180609/crew-sc-1-red-bulls-1--crew-settles-for-tie-remains-unbeaten-in-nine-games

22   Dylan Butler, "Trapp game: Columbus Crew SC captain wins AT&T Goal of the Week," *MLS website, mlssoccer.com*, published July 26, 2018, accessed September 9, 2018, https://www.mlssoccer.com/post/2018/07/26/trapp-game-columbus-crew-sc-captain-wins-att-goal-week

23   Andrew Das, *"Wayne Rooney in Talks to Leave Everton for M.L.S.,"* *The New York Times*, published May 10, 2018, accessed July 22, 2018, https://www.nytimes.com/2018/05/10/sports/soccer/wayne-rooney-dc-united-mls.html

24   Alicia DelGallo, "Star striker Dom Dwyer signs new contract with Orlando City," *Orlando Sentinel*, published January 3, 2018, accessed July 28, 2018, http://www.orlandosentinel.com/sports/orlando-city-lions/on-the-pitch/os-sp-orlando-city-dom-dwyer-new-contract-20180103-story.html

25   Ibid.

26   ESPN Staff, "Andre Blake of Philadelphia Union wins MLS Goalkeeper of the Year," *ESPN*, published November 17, 2016, accessed July 29, 2018, http://www.espn.com/soccer/philadelphia-union/story/2998210/andre-blake-of-philadelphia-union-wins-mls-goalkeeper-of-the-year

27   CBC News, "TFC home opener loss hasn't stopped fans from dreaming of back-to-back-championships," *CBC*, published March 3, 2018, accessed August 3, 2018, https://www.cbc.ca/news/canada/toronto/tfc-home-opener-1.4561409

28   Ibid.

29   Joe Prince-Wright, "Zlatan Ibrahimovic to stay in MLS but leave LA Galaxy?" *NBC Sports*, published September 22, 2018, accessed September 22, 2018, https://soccer.nbcsports.com/2018/09/22/zlatan-ibrahimovic-to-stay-in-mls-but-leave-la-galaxy/

30   Kevin Baxter, "Struggling Galaxy will be missing Ibrahimovic against streaking Seattle," *Los Angeles Times*, published August 17, 2018, accessed August 18, 2018, http://www.latimes.com/sports/soccer/la-sp-galaxy-20180817-story.html

31   Kevin Baxter, "LAFC-Galaxy game marred by vandalism and altercations," *Los Angeles Times*, published July 27, 2018, accessed August 9, 2018, http://www.latimes.com/sports/soccer/la-sp-lafc-galaxy-vandalism-20180727-story.html

32   Eric Boehm, "Minnesotans may pay for soccer stadium after all (John Oliver says it's a bad idea)," *Watchdog.org*, published July 13, 2015, accessed July 24, 2018, https://www.watchdog.org/issues/accountability/minnesotans-may-pay-for-soccer-stadium-after-all-john-oliver/article_cff9d959-cad1-5178-b5a9-11762d729f53.html

33   Christopher Kamrani, "Real Salt Lake legend Kyle Beckerman is closer to the end than the beginning of his career – and he intends to make it count," *The Salt Lake Tribune*, published July 20, 2018, updated July 21, 2018, accessed August 24, 2018, https://www.sltrib.com/sports/rsl/2018/07/20/real-salt-lakes-kyle/

34   Maddie Lee, "As RSL tries to find its way, Mike Petke trying to expand club's leadership circle," *The Salt Lake Tribune*, published May 7, 2018, updated May 8, 2018, accessed August 24, 2018, https://www.sltrib.com/sports/rsl/2018/05/07/as-rsl-tries-to-find-its-way-mike-petke-trying-to-expand-clubs-leadership-circle/

35   Christopher Kamrani, "Real Salt Lake legend Kyle Beckerman is closer to the end than the beginning of his career – and he intends to make it count," *The Salt Lake Tribune*, published July 20, 2018, updated

July 21, 2018, accessed August 24, 2018, https://www.sltrib.com/sports/rsl/2018/07/20/real-salt-lakes-kyle/

36   Geoff Baker, "Sounders booed after failing to score again, even with man advantage, in draw with Columbus," *The Seattle Times*, published May 5, 2018, updated May 5, 2018, accessed July 31, 2018, https://www.seattletimes.com/sports/sounders/sounders-booed-after-failing-to-score-again-even-with-man-advantage-in-draw-with-columbus/

37   Tribune wire reports (Associated Press), "MLS players ratify 5-year labor contract through 2019," *Chicago Tribune*, published July 16, 2015 | Bethesda, MD., accessed September 22, 2018, http://www.chicagotribune.com/sports/soccer/ct-soccer-mls-players-labor-contract-spt-20150716-story.html

38   German Sferra, "Harpos, Rayados in Action as Southeast, Central & Mountain Qualifiers Start for 2019 U.S. Open Cup," *U.S. Soccer*, published September 14, 2018, accessed September 19, 2018, https://www.ussoccer.com/stories/2018/09/20/00/45/20190919-preview-usoc-2019-qualifying-central-mountain-and-southeast

39   Rachel Bachman, "For U.S. Men, World Cup Is a Painful Reminder," *The Wall Street Journal*, published July 8, 2018, accessed July 26, 2018, https://www.wsj.com/articles/for-u-s-men-world-cup-is-a-painful-reminder-1531047601

40   Andrew Das, "*U.S. Soccer Names Dave Sarachan to Coach Men's Team Against Portugal*," *The New York Times*, published October 24, 2017, accessed July 26, 2018, https://www.nytimes.com/2017/10/24/sports/soccer/usmnt-dave-sarachan-coach.html

CREDITS

Design & Layout
Cover and interior design: Annika Naas
Layout: Amnet
Cover photos: © AdobeStock

Editorial
Managing editor: Elizabeth Evans
Copyeditor: Anne Rumery